Sacred Dimensions
of Time and Space

SACRED DIMENSIONS OF TIME AND SPACE

Tarthang Tulku

Dharma  Publishing

TIME SPACE AND KNOWLEDGE SERIES

Time, Space, and Knowledge
Love of Knowledge
Knowledge of Time and Space
Dynamics of Time and Space
Sacred Dimensions of Time and Space

ISBN 10: 0-89800-360-1
ISBN 13: 978-0-89800-360-4

Typeset in Adobe Trump Mediaeval and Helvetica Light.
Printed and bound by Dharma Press, Berkeley, CA.

9   8   7   6   5   4   3   2

*Dedicated to the
growth of knowledge*

CONTENTS

TIME

KNOWLEDGE

Publisher's
Preface

Two decades ago, Dharma Publishing published a new book by Tarthang Tulku, *Time, Space, and Knowledge: A New Vision of Reality*. From its first page, this remarkable work introduced an unusual style of inquiry and a truly unique vision. We were not surprised, when scientists, educators, psychologists, systems theorists, and independent thinkers from all walks of life acknowledged *Time, Space, and Knowledge (TSK)* as a pathbreaking work.

Soon workshops and long-term programs on *TSK*, led by students of Tarthang Tulku, were being organized in several countries. In 1980, the first of several volumes of essays inspired by the TSK vision was published, and translations began to appear. In the decade after its publication, *TSK* was adopted for classroom use in more than a hundred colleges and universities. Word of *TSK* spread from reader to reader, and the demand for *TSK* has remained steady ever since.

The continuing interest in TSK, coupled with many requests for more material on the vision, encouraged Tarthang Tulku to continue his inquiry into time, space, and knowledge. In 1987, we published *Love of Knowledge*, followed in 1990 by *Knowledge of Time and Space*. In 1993 came *Visions of Knowledge*, and in 1994 *Dynamics of Time and Space*. Each of these works revealed the endless riches that this way of exploring our human nature offered, and each demonstrated the remarkable creativity and playfulness that the vision seemed able to inspire.

Now Dharma Publishing is extremely pleased to present the fifth volume in the TSK series, *Sacred Dimensions of Time and Space*. Everyone connected with its production has had a similar response: great enthusiasm for this utterly fresh and stimulating presentation, together with gratitude to Tarthang Tulku for continuing to make works of so much power and value available. Those of us familiar with the heavy workload he carries in other areas can only marvel that he is able to present such a gift.

Early readers of *Sacred Dimensions of Time and Space* have uniformly been inspired and uplifted by reading this work. Dharma Publishing has already made tentative plans for a follow-up publication in the Perspectives on TSK series, in which readers can pursue some of the issues that this major new work raises.

For everyone at Dharma Publishing, the efforts through the years to prepare the books of the TSK series for publication have been deeply rewarding. Most gratifying, however, has been the clear sense that readers find these works to be of unusual value. We regularly hear from individuals all over the world who contact us to express their appreciation for the TSK vision.

It gives us great delight to think of the joy with which our old friends will greet this new publication. And we look forward as well to the hosts of new readers *Sacred Dimensions of Time and Space* seems certain to attract. May people everywhere benefit from the continuing presentation of the TSK vision.

Preface

Acquiring knowledge is like breathing: We are born knowing how to do it. We come into the world with our senses primed and a mind eager to know. From these shared capacities have arisen the great civilizations and countless achievements of humanity.

Today the world is filled with the knowledge that the efforts of human beings have brought into being. Each culture, each knowledge discipline, each individual contributes to a fantastically complex mosaic, its parts constantly shifting, interacting, and taking new forms.

But times are changing. The very developments that have made us aware as never before of the wealth of human knowledge are also blurring distinctions and wiping out whole ways of knowing. For better or worse, we are moving toward a global culture.

In the past, different communities lived in relative isolation, and cultures would arise and pass away in time like beautiful flowers that bloom and then fade away, leaving no trace. Today all this has changed. Regions once remote in space are now in steady communication. It is as though great mountain ranges that once separated isolated valleys had crumbled away. Everything is jumbled together; everything is in constant transition. In the midst of this upheaval, our ever accumulating knowledge of the past is of little use, for the structures that gave order then seem largely irrelevant now.

As cultures meet and merge, the mosaic begins to look less like a harmonious design and more like chaos. The flowers that once gave pleasure through their beauty now vie for space, choking each other off, until every plant becomes another weed in an impenetrable thicket.

By some measures, the growth of knowledge in this century has been explosive, inconceivable by the standards of an earlier age. But as information accumulates, there is also a growing sense that knowledge has become pointless, or that certain fundamental kinds of knowledge have been lost. Without a sheltering framework of meaning and significance, knowledge becomes dead facts: data to be filed away and retrieved when it seems useful.

Clearly there is no turning back, no way to restore the frameworks that human beings once relied on to sustain a fundamental sense of well-being. But as borders break down, a new openness emerges. Could this openness sustain us? Could it offer a very different kind of support?

The collapse of old structures also has a liberating effect on knowledge. No longer bound to specifics, knowledge is free to operate at a different level, to bring out the benefits of being alive in space and time. Amidst our confusion and uncertainty, we can sense this possibility. Knowledge is in the mood to move!

At present we live in a strange, in-between kind of world. We have lost the sense of stable truths that can guide human destiny, but we continue to be bound by the conviction that our knowledge has fixed limits. In one sense, we are trapped in this awkward place, forced there by the logic of our knowing. But no one is imposing these structures upon us. We are doing it ourselves, and if we determine to change, we are free to do so. We are knowledgeable beings, and knowledge can retrain knowledge.

In times of turbulence such as ours, the risk is great that knowledge will be rejected entirely, or else misunderstood as consisting of facts and opinions, in which case it will become ideology and dogma. But the open dynamic of our times presents us with another option. Because we do not know where we are headed, because the old certainties are gone, because time and space themselves are in flux, we can turn to knowledge expectantly. If we welcome knowledge and invite it into our lives, we can draw inspiration from our own capacity to know. Exercising knowledge, we can allow its intrinsic vitality to transform our presuppositions, invigorating every field of inquiry and each tradition and transcending all limits. Confident in the power of knowledge to bring real benefit, we can foster creation of the Body of Knowledge.

Conventional knowledge today focuses on the self: what the self needs, what it understands, what it is capable of. Suppose that we shift this focus, looking in a more neutral way at how our being functions. As sentient beings we are alive in space and time, and we draw on knowledge to give meaning to experience. When we place these three factors—space, time, and knowledge—at the center of our being, something quite remarkable happens. Knowledge comes into its own, informing experience and existence in a very powerful way.

The promise of the Time, Space, Knowledge vision—TSK—is this: If we understand our own space more fully, we can open all of space. If we know our own time more intimately, we can transform our living experience. If we investigate the operations of our own mind more deeply, we can see the roots of knowledge everywhere. Seeing the natural harmony within appearance, we will be able to take advantage of the extraordinary opportunity time is steadily presenting.

The starting point for such transformation is to investigate time, space, and knowledge in our own experience, challenging the restrictive ways that we have learned to think of them. Such an inquiry leads us to recast our problems and obstacles as the outcome of how we understand and embody time and space and knowledge. And this recognition in turn allows us to experience the benefits that flow from a different vision.

Once we open to this vision, the growing closeness of space need not confine knowledge, nor need the intensifying speed of time pressure it. We can open the edges of forms in space, and we can make the momentum of time our own. Distinctions made by ordinary knowledge have brought us this far in our history. Now is the time to open to a new level of knowledge, one where inclusion is more natural than exclusion and synthesis is more creative than separation.

In such a way of being, boundaries become transparent to light. Light informs light, reflecting and enriching the world, revealing hidden dimensions of beauty, joy and love. As our horizons brighten, we understand that we are part of time, space, and knowledge, that they share in our being. Turning naturally toward the light, we see in all directions the glow of new knowledge, manifesting in warm and radiant colors. Eventually a new sun of knowledge dawns, revealing space without barriers, time beyond measure, and knowledge that is free from all discrimination.

The deep tranquility of space can calm our bodies and suffuse our minds. Attuned to space, we see that we are linked to all appearance. The gift of this gentle intimacy allows knowledge to arise effortlessly, inseparable from wonder at the magical play of manifestation. Time itself becomes spacious and expansive, inviting us to dance and play, leading us toward unawaited treasures.

As these transitions deepen, we find that we are at home with our own embodiment, with our own senses and our own thoughts. Our hearts experience the unspeakable beauty of appearance. We see that we can participate more fully in being, opening whatever is closed and melting whatever is rigid. The grace and wonder of creation in space and time become available.

Space, time, and knowledge are universal, and at the same time they are intensely 'my own'. No one is a stranger to their manifestation, and no one holds the secret key to their working. Since that is so, dogma and beliefs, territory and exclusion have no role to play. Whoever develops knowledge, whatever form it takes, is participating in the time-space-knowledge that shape our being—contributing to the dynamic of the whole.

The TSK approach promotes an inquiry broad enough to explore our participation in space, and powerful enough to penetrate time's mysteries. It invites us to explore the sacred dimensions of time and space. And it reveals that knowledge itself, known and unknown, familiar and unimagined, is sacred in its power to shape our reality and make available unending benefits. May this discovery, which each of us is free to make, contribute to the well-being of the world.

Tarthang Tulku
Odiyan, California
December 1997

Orientation

Time and space offer beauty beyond measure and power beyond reckoning. When knowledge can free itself from the barriers to understanding that we have imposed, we know this to be so. Within each point of time or space infinite depths are available. In the field of space, the potential for transforming insight beckons, inviting us to claim our rightful inheritance.

Long ago—perhaps when we were children, or perhaps when the human race was still young—we chose a way of knowing that put time and space at a distance. Ever since, we have structured our lives accordingly.

Yet the narrow line we choose to walk, the tunnel into which we compress our being, does not fit our experience or our capacities. Our lives are filled with countless reminders that time and space are more than we imagine. Despite the limiting identities we assign, the radiance of being shines through. The moment we look, a different kind of knowledge is available.

The Time Space Knowledge vision (TSK) initiates an inquiry that invokes our own inborn capacity to know. It asks us to take full responsibility for the knowledge we live by and the choices through which we shape our lives. TSK introduces us to the sacred symbols of time and space, which have the power to reveal the whole of knowledge to the whole of mind.

TSK engages the knowledge that guides us, the time that offers us opportunity, and the space that allows us to participate in reality. The more we understand how these three elements interact, the more the limits we have learned to take for granted dissolve. We do not have to proceed step by step; we can turn reality around . . . just like that! This freedom is our birthright.

At present we are bound to a particular understanding of space and time, one that makes certain limits seem very real. For instance, we accept that time unfolds from one moment to the next, that our thoughts can only move from one type of thing to another in a predictable sequence, and that specific events invariably take a fixed length of time. The idea that we could experience an hour in a single minute seems sheer nonsense.

Similarly, while everyone agrees that space can accommodate a vast range of appearance, we do not ask how to benefit from that allowing. We know that there is no going outside space, but we do not see the presence of space everywhere as an offer and an invitation. We assume that space operates in certain well-defined ways. But who has set these limits? Could there be space within space? What if we discovered that vast realms can fit into very small enclosures?

Such examples could be multiplied. We think in terms of 'here' and 'there', divide time into past, present, and future, and classify knowledge into known and unknown. Intent on sizing up what appears in terms of its characteristics, we forget to notice that form itself depends on both time and space. Determined to use knowledge to our own advantage, we fail to ask whether there are ways of knowing that operate beyond our claims of ownership.

In our present way of understanding, time and space recede into the background. Yet time and space are more than just the background for appearance and experience, and also more than special sorts of 'things'. They are the partners whose dance whirls existence into being. Knowing that, we step into a different world.

DIALOGUE OF BEING

Fortunately, space and time are not affected by our attempts to tame them, nor is knowledge cut off from appearance when we fail to acknowledge it. This ongoing availability of time and space and knowledge lies at the heart of the TSK vision.

TSK invites us to see ourselves as an expression of time, space, and knowledge. This suggestion will seem surprising until we actually begin to put it into effect. Then we start to notice the restricted patterns that presently shape our lives, and to understand the patterned dynamic that has set them in place. As insight moves from the realm of theory to actual embodiment, remarkable possibilities open.

The key to activating the vision is inquiry. We can use imagination, visualization, speculation, common sense—whatever helps to sharpen our questions and awaken our intelligence. Good questions are an invitation to knowledge to sit at our table as our honored guest. Having accepted our invitation, knowledge brings with it time and space. If we treat all three with appreciation and respect, they soon begin to speak among themselves, giving us the rare privilege of listening in.

Inspired by the ongoing dialogue of time, space, and knowledge, inquiry deepens of its own accord. New knowledge arises, and while we are not its authors, we can certainly be grateful participants, joining in as creative vision and dynamic action begin to manifest. If the invitation we have extended is genuine, and if we hold it open by vigorously exercising the knowledge already available to us, there seem no limits on what knowledge can do and where it can lead us.

Multifaceted inquiry has a vast, transforming effect. Space grows more spacious, and seems infused with light. Its countless dimensions easily accommodate mind, easing the tensions that thoughts and emotions so readily accumulate. Responding to the openness of space, time begins to show us new faces. We discover we can find ways to enter into the rhythms that move beneath the surface of time's linear directionality. In turn, a knowledge attuned to space and time is able to command appearance differently. Our human problems may become much more workable.

All this happens of its own accord. It is as though space has been holding open the door, time has been waiting for us to dive in more deeply, and knowledge has patiently held itself available until the moment we are ready to ask. Now that time has come. Now we can enjoy the freedom that is our birthright.

SETTING KNOWLEDGE FREE

If each of us embodies time, space, and knowledge, why must we make special efforts to activate that embodiment? The answer is that we have adopted a narrow approach toward knowledge, turning it into a prized possession. But our attempts to hold on to knowledge have a paradoxical effect. Instead of opening freely, knowledge is cut off, forced into tight corners.

Each of us learns to seize on certain fundamental facts as true, and these become our body of knowledge. But because we cling so tightly to this treasure of knowledge, we may distort it. At the least, we cut off its capacity to grow and take on new forms.

Suppose that the inspiration of new knowledge convinced us to open our clenched hand and let knowledge go free. Would we have lost anything? Or would knowledge at last be able to celebrate its own power, shifting and metamorphosing into something far more splendid than we had been able to possess?

One way to set knowledge free is to rethink the most simple and fundamental questions: Who am I?

What am I doing on this earth? How shall I use my time? It is easy enough to come up with answers in words—even TSK words. For instance, we could say: "I am knowledge . . . I am time . . . I am space." But these are just words. Can we question the one who gives those answers? Can we question how to question? Can we invite time and space to give the answers?

In TSK, it is questioning that matters, for answers are just one more thing to hold on to tightly. Questioning loosens our grip on the presupposed. Each time our questions bring an assumption into the light of inquiry, we experience the sense of freedom that comes with greater access to time, space, and knowledge. Questions let us test our experience and challenge the structures we take for granted. Through questioning, we enact a vision of time, space, and knowledge as the great guardians of being.

The TSK vision invites us to initiate our own questioning, and to judge for ourselves how valuable such inquiry can be. That is the whole of its message. Once the qualities of knowingness are in operation, the clarity at which philosophy aims, the radiant purity that inspires ethical conduct, and the penetrating certainty sought in religious traditions develop of their own accord as an outpouring of vitality and sensitivity.

In TSK, knowledge is primary. The growth of knowledge automatically promotes all disciplines and fulfills all goals. Once we learn to set it free, knowledge can celebrate its own capacity, quickly transcending the structures of repetition on which we so often rely.

QUESTIONING AS KNOWLEDGE

T hroughout human history, there has been a tendency to try to capture knowledge in the form of labels, words, and specific belief systems. But such structures, useful though they may be as tools, do not do justice to knowledge. Systems of belief are the tracks that knowledge leaves behind. If we substitute them for knowledge itself, they begin to proliferate, crowding out a deeper knowing and the inspiration it can bring. When this pattern is operating, creating an opening for real knowledge to enter will require tremendous effort.

Questioning and open inquiry offer a far more immediate approach to knowledge. When we question our own experience and the nature of what appears, we let knowledge inspire and bring alive what time and space present. When this dynamic has been engaged, knowledge develops freely of its own accord, and life becomes far richer.

When knowledge is understood as the specific beliefs and convictions we happen to consider true, the value of questioning can easily be misunderstood. From such a perspective, it may make sense not to question what seems well-established, not to risk the destruction of what has been carefully constructed. Knowledge has taken on a substance of its own, and the integrity of this construct must be preserved.

The TSK response to such concerns is a renewed invitation to inquiry, to awaken a different kind of knowledge. If there are truly limits on what the human mind can know, we need not fear coming up against them. But if those limits are self-imposed, if they arise out of convictions whose origins remain obscure, it seems wrong to cut off inquiry. Why settle for less than might be possible? Why not explore the alternatives?

Whatever we know or experience as real is also an object of human knowledge. Since we have named it, we know that it depends on the naming power of the mind; since we experience it, we know that it arises out of our ability to interact with whatever appears. In other words, reality as we know it must reflect our own capacity for knowledge. This does not mean that the mind creates reality, but it does mean that mind and what the mind knows are inseparable.

In that case, could the mind know differently? Simply leaving this as an open question gives inquiry the scope it needs. By inquiring, we get feedback from our inquiry, allowing us to refine our questions. The answers we arrive at and hypotheses we pursue may prove inaccurate, but as long as we do not seize on these answers as the truth, that is a secondary concern. Mistaken views can also be the foundation for growth and new perspectives. Like time, knowledge has its own dynamic. As it changes through time, it also grows, allowing for transformation.

TSK is not concerned with adding to the positions and definitions that make up the standard body of knowledge. Even its most surprising—or plausible— theories and hypotheses should be heard as specula-tions, as invitations to inquiry rather than pronounce-ments about what is so. Nor does TSK ask us to abandon the beliefs we may have developed. It is no friend of an easy skepticism or cynicism. Instead, TSK asks us to look for the knowledge *within* conventional knowledge—the knowledge that founds our beliefs and certifies our convictions.

The TSK approach is like adding a catalyst to a chemical reaction: Suddenly things that had long lain dormant began to fizz and bubble, sending off bursts of light and energy. Solids melt away, revealing time, space, and knowledge at work. We awaken our own intelligence and discover something fundamental about our own being.

Like anything else put into words, TSK can become a set of beliefs or a methodology—one that some people possess and others do not. There is nothing surprising in this, for history shows that human beings love to lay claim and incorporate; to insist on their identities, their ownership, and their being 'right'. For TSK, however, such an approach is deadly. If TSK is established as a system or an 'ism', it loses its power to free time and space from the 'truth' of what we already know to be so. Then the ongoing boycott of knowledge will continue in operation.

To deal with this danger, TSK requires our full participation. Can we strengthen knowledge through our questioning? Can we invite it into the innermost part of our own lives? Can we pound on the 'is' of each 'ism' and question each establishment?

Once we commit ourselves to knowledge—to exploring it, allowing it to open, and sharing it with others—knowledge itself will do the rest. Focusing on our own experience, our own awareness and thoughts, our own embodiment, we create the conditions for mind to unite with space and time. We can relax our demanding, allowing the fullness of space to open and the dynamic of time to emerge.

No Mystery

Ordinary knowledge works within a standard framework, which we might call the logos. The logos itself, since it frames and shapes what ordinary knowledge takes for granted, could be considered a form of higher knowledge. Yet the structure of the logos seems to perpetuate a form of understanding in which knowledge 'belongs' to someone or something. When this happens, when knowledge becomes a possession, there will be identification and identity. Knowledge will go toward the given, and restrictions will stay in place.

The framework of the logos, when it is visible at all, tends to be off-limits to inquiry. As for those central beliefs that the logos identifies—reality, process, linear time, a first cause, the identity of the self—as long as the logos remains in operation, there is no way to call these into question. When challenges come, the logos turns shy. Strangely inarticulate, it appeals to the ineffable, to mysteries that knowledge cannot fathom. If this approach fails, it turns defensive or scornful.

For TSK, however, every unexplained mystery is a fruitful point for inquiry. Perhaps the mystery is real;

perhaps there is nothing to say. But until we have asked for ourselves, why accept that this is so?

A good example is our ordinary understanding of time. Although we all take time for granted, we cannot easily explain how it operates. For instance, does time have a first moment? Either answer, yes or no, leads us into difficulty. How do moments of time connect to one another; how does the transition from one moment to the next occur? How does time interact with space? How are the two introduced to one another?

Such questions are usually dismissed out of hand, but perhaps that can change. In the confusion of our age, people are hungry for knowledge, and they accept the idea that knowledge changes; that what we see as true today may not be true tomorrow. In such an environment, TSK inquiry can flourish. As we wrestle with our own beliefs, aiming at clarity and encompassing vision, something fundamental may shift.

When knowledge asks new questions, space itself expands. In this more spacious realm, time slows down. In this new time frame, mind can operate differently. The logos itself comes more fully into view. Certain kinds of mysteries may dissolve.

THREE LEVELS OF TIME, SPACE, AND KNOWLEDGE

As an organizing principle for an inquiry into time, space, and knowledge, it can help to think in terms of three different levels. The first level starts from our common, everyday views of how these facets of our being operate. Do the views we hold make sense? How well do they support us in our aspirations and our activities? What are the consequences of operating with this kind of understanding? And what is the link between common-sense views and the more specialized (and possibly competing) views developed in various disciplines such as philosophy and science?

For instance, our usual view of time-space-knowledge commits us to physical existence, clock time, and knowledge linked to thoughts, concepts, and the accumulation of data. The consequence is that we find ourselves subject to sequences of cause and effect that we are powerless to change. We adopt ideas such as "better than" or "lower than," and let such distinctions introduce conflict and discord. We seek answers that accord with our initial understandings, and thus close down more far-reaching alternatives. We pursue a kind of progress that may not be progress at all.

Trapped in this way of understanding, we can only accept or reject, determine or remain ignorant. Much of the time, we choose ignorance, and then play out the consequences of this choice. And we are so thoroughly caught up in all this that we do not even realize that we are setting limits in place, or see clearly the full repercussions of the choices we have made.

The TSK vision points out these patterns and asks how solid and firmly established they are. Simply by identifying ordinary time-space-knowledge as 'first-level', it challenges the implicit assumption that there is no other way to be. It asks us not to close down prematurely the possibility of a more comprehensive and fulfilling knowledge, grounded in a different relationship to time and space. Though we feel like the black sheep of ignorance, we may yet discover the friendship of knowledge.

In suggesting a second level of time, space, and knowledge, TSK departs from standard attempts to improve our situation. Instead of asking us to change the framework or focal setting through which we currently understand our ways of being, it invites us to see the world in a new light. Thus, second-level knowledge sees space as pervasive, encompassing all appearance without ever appearing 'as' something. Likewise, it sees time as unified, going in all directions instead of unfolding along the line that marks off past from present from future. Finally, it sees existence as the union of time and space: the presence of reality.

This way of seeing offers something new—not because it is superior to prevailing systems of knowledge or belief, but because it steps outside the framework within which such systems arise and develop their perspectives. That is why TSK is not concerned with praise and blame, hope and fear, or right and wrong. It can be naturally accommodating of every alternative, because it has no position to defend or point to make. In fact, a second-level TSK perspective makes it easy to transform or transcend such dichotomies, for it reveals the mechanisms of their arising.

On the other hand, the transition to the second level does not mean that knowledge becomes remote from ordinary concerns. The intimacy with time and space that second-level knowledge brings gives a new way of dealing with fundamental human concerns, the same ones addressed by traditional religion, psychology, or any of the current models for finding meaning and value in life. When we are part of time, space, and knowledge, experience deepens naturally into joy. Space is all the therapy we need, and time directs us naturally toward fulfilling our destiny.

Looking at this second level from a first-level perspective, it is natural to ask for more specifics. To what does TSK give us access? But the question cannot be answered on its own terms. How can we describe what has previously been unavailable? The bridge has been washed away; the vehicle that would take us to the other side has not been built. This inability to describe second-level 'realities' in first-level terms follows directly from the conviction that the fundamental qualities of time, space, and knowledge available to us as human beings are fixed—that we have no choice but to live with ignorance, suffering, and error. From a second-level perspective, the real question for first-level knowledge is why such limits should operate. Is that the truth of who we are? Or do we have something better to do with our lives?

One way to suggest what second-level time, space, and knowledge offer is to say that there is a 'prior' to ignorance and suffering; that knowledge is always available to add value to our lives and introduce the chance for virtue, meaning, and joy. A second-level presentation of TSK aims to invoke this power of knowledge by loosening up the givens of first-level time and space and engaging knowledge directly. Aware that higher-level knowledge cannot be directly introduced in first-level terms, it relies on inspiration and imagination as vehicles for transformation.

At a certain level, human limits seem fixed. Our senses are restricted, our thoughts cannot encompass the whole of experience, our bodies and minds falter and grow frail. But TSK tells us we can go beyond what is repeatable, reductionist, and self-contradictory; beyond chaos, disorder, and the mindless destruction of knowledge. With a healthy attitude and a commitment to inquiry, we can become candidates for knowledge. We can judge more accurately the value of our own actions, perceptions, and thoughts.

In TSK, there is no path to such transformation. Instead, there is the availability of second-level time, space, and knowledge. By choosing the openness of space and the dynamic of time, knowledge returns to the prior. It is a journey that sets no goal, other than to embody space and time directly. Perhaps as more individuals undertake this journey, their mutual efforts will help clear the way for something new in human history to emerge.

Beyond this kind of transformation, we could speak of a third level of time, space, and knowledge. But there is little to be said. Although at this level the vision presents itself freely, it is not particularly concerned with making sense or bringing benefit. Instead, a three-part dialogue between time, space, and knowledge unfolds, inviting us to respond in kind. And so we do, expressing knowledge in our efforts to understand, time in our going along, and space in the ways that we shape what is said.

At the third-level, we are the knowledge-holders, but not the knowledge-owners. Second-level time, space, and knowledge offer an opening and a development, and that itself is the third level. It is the beauty that knowledge makes available freely, the dynamic within all difference, the opportunity for perfect embodiment. Whatever has been closed opens: The rose bud blossoms into perfection and love embraces appearance. We become master players at every game, and know all the rules by heart. We celebrate and embody. It is a journey worth the effort.

Could this analysis into levels help us understand some of the obstacles we encounter as human beings? If there are three levels for time, space, and knowledge, this gives nine levels in all, and if these levels can interact with one another in different ways, this gives twenty-seven possible combinations. Could we analyze our own experience in terms of such patternings? For instance, if an individual has a second-level orientation toward space but a first-level way of interacting with time and knowledge, what characteristic issues and attitudes will manifest? What might be a good approach to opening up the patterns that this combination tends to introduce? Studying these patterns, can we see likely places of weakness or confusion? Can we see where experience will be most intensive, or most stuck, and how it might be possible to 're-pattern' a given patterning? If there are twenty-seven patterns, are there also twenty-seven different ways of studying TSK?

ACTIVATING KNOWLEDGE

First-level knowledge is bound by the structures it identifies and put in place. For instance, knowledge must be acquired by a knower who 'goes somewhere' to get it. There is no way around this presupposition, no way out.

That is why simply identifying other possibilities for knowledge is so deeply important. Inspired by such a prospect, knowledge looks more closely at the structures it relies on and identifies. It is like looking at experience under a magnifying glass: We can see more clearly, and there is more power to our seeing.

At this point, we are still at the first level. The next step is to find another source of illumination. It is as though we discovered that we could use our magnifying glass to concentrate the rays of the sun. We all know what can happen in that case: The light may grow so intense that it causes the object under the glass to burst into flames.

Perhaps we could imagine something similar happening as knowledge intensifies. In our case, however, the flame would not consume its object, but instead reveal it in a new and transfiguring light.

In one sense, however, our analogy is false. The transition to a second-level inquiry does not require finding a new source of knowledge. Instead, knowledge transforms itself *as we exercise it*. The more we bring knowledge to bear, the more knowledge reveals its own value. For knowledge knows what to do.

Whatever our initial view of the benefits that might result from such a transformation, we find that the fruits of inquiry are far greater than what we had imagined. Knowledge makes us a gift of knowledge, initiating a cycle of growth whose potential is inexpressible.

Exercising knowledge activates the dialogue of time, space, and knowledge. Presently time and space speak only of limits. "You have to go," says time; "You cannot do," says space. But when time and space are free to speak for themselves and with each other, they communicate a very different message. Now the words they have for us are healing. They reveal new possibilities—new ways to end our isolation and the territoriality it brings; new sources for experience that unite joy with beauty and dynamic creativity. We can join in this dialogue, letting knowledge speak naturally in all we do.

In all our actions and every thought, we can embody time and space and celebrate knowledge. We can see the infinite value and beauty in every human endeavor. Like others who have made knowledge into a profession or discipline, we can cultivate knowledge, without letting it become rigid or restrictive. Knowledge can be our good friend, sharing with us all that is has to offer. It can be our inner environment: the truth we aim at and the aspirations through which we shape our lives.

When we understand knowledge at this level, we see that the countless views and doctrines that have emerged through history are all expressions of knowledge, the footprints that knowledge makes as it travels through time and space. The fact that they go in different directions should not make us think that they lead toward contradiction and opposition, any more than the blossoming of flowers in the field or the profusion of stars in the sky lead to contradiction. Through the inspiration of knowledge, countless forms have taken shape, countless distinctions and ratios. Only when knowledge is used to erect borders does diversity lead to conflict; only when space and time are turned into something rigid does opposition develop.

Whenever knowledge takes form, limits emerge. But if we see the countless expressions of knowledge as dynamic variations, each of them becomes a pointer toward the unrevealed depths where a deeper knowing is available. In these depths, knowledge is freely available. We move toward knowledge effortlessly.

PROMISE OF KNOWLEDGE

Our lives are shaped by the emerging and interaction of finite points in time and space. Engaging this emerging reality, we too are intent on making our point. Yet do we know how the point took form? Do we understand the baseline from which our lives take shape? Can we say how past, present, and future are connected? Express the meaning of experience? Do we understand the nature and significance of transitions?

For each and every one of us, the starting point for conducting an inquiry into such questions is what is happening here and now, with our own embodiment, own motives and concerns, and our own ways of knowing. We are all free to explore in our own way, using the tools and materials at hand. There is no need to discard or clarify wrong notions or mistaken understanding before we begin: We can simply set forth. Any kind of knowledge contributes to our 'here', and all ways of understanding can serve as a starting point.

As soon as we begin to look at our starting point from different angles, it opens up. We see distinctions, relationships, and ratios that were not available before. The very shape of our questions begins to reflect greater knowledge. And for its part, knowledge, freed from the restrictions that we have artificially imposed on it, just keeps growing.

A fitting symbol for this quality of availability is light. In its shining, light manifests a rhythm and motion that engage time, and its illumination is central to the allowingness of space. Without light, there can be no perception and reflection, and thus no knowledge. Our personal understanding depends on the operation of light: light reflecting light back to light. The quality of illumination is the point of being, and the point of being is the time-space-knowledge trinity.

Seeing this to be so, we discover the beautiful exhibition of knowledge, ever available. We realize that the play of time, space, and knowledge manifests in every star that shines at night. We understand that our present being, our past mistakes, and our finest future potential are all united with the whole of appearance. We recognize that all civilizations, all religions, all great leaders inspired to new vision and accomplishment, draw on the power of knowledge commanding space and time.

The perfection of knowledge in time and space could be understood as the perfection of human being. But such perfection is not a process that comes to an end, not a completion. It never stops, and so it never fails. Throughout space and time, in all directions, knowledge is available. When that is so for us, we unite with being, and arrive at the fullness of human being.

The vision presented here could be considered a saying of our being by time, space, and knowledge, presented from within the fullness they evoke. Our task is to allow it to speak clearly, listening with open appreciation. Once the saying is complete, however, anyone is free to offer feedback, make interpretations, draw conclusions, find applications. For that is the final truth of human being. We are free to proceed in our own way.

Sacred Dimensions
of Time and Space

S PACE allows and accommodates. It invites all form to appear as its guest, free from discrimination.

TIME brings alive what has taken shape and form. It presents the dynamic of unfolding, the momentum of creation. The union of time with space becomes the being of the point, the availability of 'here'.

KNOWLEDGE brings the point to fullness. Making, taking, granting, and establishing, knowledge points out. The depth of knowledge discloses the depth of the point, allowing existence to enter the fullness of being.

At present, space is used up in establishing the distance from here to there. Time is exhausted in getting from here to there. Knowledge is restricted to pointing out the here, the there, and the distance between them.

Yet within these limits, the depth of being is available. The power of knowledge sets forth, the dynamic of time transforms, and the openness of space allows.

Appearance and experience are gateways to these depths. They open the sacred dimensions of being.

Introduction

The knowledge that seems most self-evident is this: 'I am here'. Suppose we make this knowledge our starting point. Can we let this fundamental axiom of first-level knowledge open into deeper, more penetrating knowledge? Can we awaken a curiosity about the significance of this statement, which so strongly sets in place a personal understanding of what knowledge is all about? If we let the knowledge that 'I am here' expresses speak, what does it have to tell us?

In 'I am here', we can take 'I' as the point of view operating at this particular point, 'am' as being alive in time 'now', and 'here' as the zero-point in space from which we begin. So far we have a zero-dimensional world, a zero-point that manifests not only in space, but also in time and in knowledge. But a point 'here' makes little sense without another point 'there', and making this connection also gives us a baseline between these two points. Now there is subject and object, self and world, knower and known. Interestingly, this simple shape—a line marked off by two identified locations, could be seen as the letter 'I' turned on edge, and this letter (in English, the language of this inquiry), designates the point of view of the self. Perhaps we can take this as a message from knowledge, an indication that our line of inquiry may prove fruitful.

In identifying 'here' and 'there' and the baseline between them, we have assumed that these two points can be located. But to locate along the line requires another structure off the line, one that intersects the line at a specified place. Thus, a zero-point is typically located at the juncture of an x-axis with a y-axis, two lines that serve to specify the location of the point. However, the axes themselves, considered as structures, depend on four end-points, and each of these four points will require its own locating axes. In this way we arrive at sixteen points in all. When we explore the structure we have set in place in other ways (for instance, by bringing in the baseline and the 'there', or by treating the zero-point as three-dimensional), we arrive in each case at sixteen. Let us take this sixteen to indicate completion.

When we consider the movement along the baseline from 'here' to 'there', we find that the zero-point can also be opened up along the axes. If the zero-point is not non-dimensional, this opening will be a radiating out, in the shape of a cone. Such cones can be generated along lines in each of sixteen directions. Having emerged from zero, the face of each cone (which is also the 'there') remains zero; thus, each zero gives rise to sixteen zeros.

This whole construction, based on the 'I am here' as zero-point, remains fully reducible to zero. Without the zero-point, no lines or cones can develop; at the same time, until lines have been generated, zero cannot be located, and the cones that give rise to further zero-points cannot emerge. Since each line can potentially be analyzed into zeros, we could consider the whole of this interdependent structure a reflection of zero.

Nonetheless, the 'basis' generated in this way makes it possible to establish a viewpoint, and also to identify, measure, and describe qualities. In other words, it makes possible the activities of knowledge and the arising of forms that make themselves available to be known. What is more, the simplicity of the structure means that form can readily duplicate itself in all directions, creating intricate structures built up through radiating cones and zero-point spheres.

We have no basis for calling this zero-point structure 'true', but we also have no reason to call it false. In any case, such conclusions seem secondary. What matters is that such a structure allows for a very far-reaching inquiry into the operations of time, space, and knowledge, one not bound to the usual assumptions that tend to close down questioning in advance. And because this inquiry is founded in 'I am here', it is one that any 'I' can make. Although it is 'my' inquiry, it belongs to no one.

Perhaps this unusual structure can grant knowledge unusual access. Perhaps it will allow us to listen more closely as knowledge speaks. For although at one level time, space, and knowledge must remain unaffected by the lines and marks we make to divide or organize them, knowledge could also be said to respond to the measures we take. In the structure sketched out above, the particular forms identified, together with their interconnections, allow us to explore shape, character, form, substance, distance, direction, motion, dimension, change, continuity, rhythms, transitions, observation, perceptions, conceptions—in short, the fundamental elements that make up the world that time, space, and knowledge present. The present work is a record of one such set of explorations.

OBJECTIVE AND SUBJECTIVE

As a starting point for inquiry, the zero-point can be investigated equally well in terms of space or time or knowledge. However, since we begin with the 'I am here', it seems natural to place special emphasis on the zero-point as the subjective knower, the 'I' whose existence seems to us so certain.

Does a focus on the *subjective* knower mean giving up on the possibility of *objective* knowledge? That would be true only if objective knowledge could be divorced from the subject who engages in the act of knowing. But this would be a faulty approach. It is a little like looking at the moon through a telescope without first determining whether the telescope is functioning properly, whether its lens has been properly ground, and whether we are sufficiently skilled to operate it. When that is our approach—when we try to observe objective reality without first understanding the process of observation and the qualities and limitations of the instruments we are using—can we really expect to get reliable results?

The 'I am here' is the lens through which we look out on the world. Suppose our lens is defective; suppose, for instance, that it induces a kind of astigmatism. Inevitably our knowledge of the world would be deficient. To our astigmatic vision, much that we saw would be enigmatic. Based on this faulty foundation, the understandings we developed would be unreliable: short-lived and liable to lead us into contradiction. As one faulty observation gave way to another, we would find ourselves mired in confusion and uncertainty.

Anyone interested in objective knowledge must face head on the possibility that we are operating under just such defective conditions, without even realizing it. Do we know how subjective knowledge works? Do we know what it takes to be a fully qualified observer? If we learned that we could improve the quality of subjective knowledge—could take it to a different level—how could we afford to pass up the opportunity?

At the same time, those who stress the importance of developing 'objective' knowledge have a point. If we focus too strongly on the concerns of the self, or let ourselves get caught up in its stories, its needs, its biases, and its predispositions, knowledge will almost certainly be obscured.

One reason the inquiry presented here may prove fruitful is that it does not attempt to move to the objective pole of knowledge too quickly, but also does not get caught up in the endless webs of first-level subjectivity. Our starting point is the 'I am here', but our method is to investigate this 'I am here', in its component parts, as the zero-point for first-level time, space, and knowledge. This approach takes us to a level where the usual structures of the self do not operate. We might say that we are conducting an objective inquiry into structures usually considered subjective, but even that is misleading, since the distinction into subjective and objective is one of the structures being investigated. Perhaps it is enough to say that we are investigating 'here' as well as 'there', that our aim is to clarify the 'from' from which our ordinary knowledge proceeds.

We could also put it very differently. In conducting the inquiry, we are simply listening to a story told by knowledge, or watching a play put on by time and presented by space. The cast of characters is rather unusual: Zero-point, axes, baseline, and cone appear early on, and sixteen and ratio have important parts to play as the drama unfolds. But this is only at one level. At another level, the actors are time, space, and knowledge, who play the role of audience as well as players. And what of 'I am here', whose story we thought we were going to hear? It too has a role to play. But it may not be the one for which it thought it was auditioning.

When our inquiry can proceed on all these levels at once, it begins to develop real power. As we see how the 'I am here' generates a cone of subjective knowledge, the very act of seeing begins to open that cone into zero. The immediate effect is to release an energy and intelligence that has been bound up in conventional structures. We are still operating at the first level of knowledge, but we have begun to put time, space, and knowledge at the center of our inquiry. There they can freely interact. From our first-level perspective the result may be a kind of explosion, a dynamic liberation of light, as being comes alive.

FOUNDATION FOR INQUIRY

How can an inquiry that starts with a kind of space-geometry lead to a new way of being? The answer may unfold more clearly as this book proceeds, but for now we can at least point toward the special qualities of space that found our inquiry.

Although the investigation conducted here applies to space and time and knowledge alike, the language of points and cones and lines that it adopts belong primarily to space. That seems only natural, for space is the background for our very existence, the precondition for our embodiment. Whatever we make of our lives, whatever we discover in the world around us, it is because space has made it available.

Space is the opening through which existence can appear and experience take place. Space allows 'here' to make contact with 'there', so that directions and dimensions become possible. We could even say that the 'there' allowed by space is a precondition for the 'here' of 'I am here'.

9

Space gives shape and form, distance and qualities. It communicates reality. The zero-point, which establishes nothing but still allows form to unfold, could be understood as a representative of this space openness. The process through which zero expands into 16, radiating forms and structures that never depart from zero, parallels the way that conventional space allows an infinite play of appearance to manifest, without ever becoming something other than space.

If we take this lead, we can investigate the 'I am here' without turning it into an abstraction. We can rely on the experience of our body and our senses: not because they give us truth about what is 'there', but because they are vital to our 'here'. We can question vigorously, but we can also appreciate what space makes available, and our appreciation can deepen into love.

When time gives space the opportunity to open in our hearts, we discover the field of space as identical with the play of time. We know that we do not have to rely on someone else's understanding or vision, but can journey into knowledge on our own.

In psychological terms, this means that life becomes more rich, and also more manageable. But this is not to say that our inquiry becomes psychological, or that we return to subjectivity after all. Instead, we recover the 'I am here' as an expression of space-time-knowledge: not an abstract proposition to be analyzed or a claim to insist on, but the truth of our being.

When we let the 'here' of 'I am here' open into the fullness of space, the juncture that presents the zero-point becomes the meeting point of time and space and knowledge, and the baseline becomes our connection with others, a link that has been there from the beginning. The space and senses and perception we ordinarily operate open differently, ready to accommodate joy. We find that we are at home in the universe.

BEAUTY OF INQUIRY

T he beauty of time-space-knowledge inquiry is that absolutely everyone shares in this same structure, and so everyone is free to question, free to grow in knowledge. Each of us is born from time-space-knowledge, and each of us is bonded to time-space-knowledge. First-level knowledge may dispute the style of inquiry we adopt or the conclusions we reach, but it seems difficult to dispute this fundamental starting point. And that is enough. For if we start from time, space, and knowledge, inquiry itself will do the rest. Space and time and knowledge themselves will be transformed.

One reason 'I am here' seems a fruitful starting point is that it clarifies this ongoing intimacy of human being with time, space, and knowledge. It invites the dialogue of time and space and knowledge to begin, and invites us all to listen in. But there are other modes of inquiry as well. Others can question differently, bringing to their investigation the precision that comes from different disciplines. Acknowledging their debt to knowledge, they can make their own contribution, sharing the fruits of their inquiry with others.

There are times in history when knowledge seems poised to open in new directions. For example, exactly 360 years ago, the French philosopher René Descartes published *Discourse on Method*, a pathbreaking work that sought to create a new basis for knowledge by starting with the existence of the 'I' as the only indisputable reality. As an appendix to that work, Descartes included a short treatise that laid out the new science of analytic geometry, which he hoped would provide a starting point for sure and precise knowledge. Though they certainly built on the work of distinguished predecessors, those two works taken together could be seen as inaugurating a new era in knowledge.

Today, when so much in our understanding of the world seems uncertain and unfounded, the time seems right for a similar breakthrough. Perhaps we can invite knowledge to step forward once again, sharing with us a new method of inquiry that can open an unparalleled investigation into our being and destiny as human beings.

It is too soon to say what form such inquiry may ultimately take. But what is presented here could be understood as one possible model. At the least, it is one way of telling the story. True, the 'I' of 'I am here' starts off liking the old way; it sees no need for a change. But as the inquiry proceeds, that first-level point of view can be recast; the story can be retold. 'I am here' is given by space and time and knowledge. Knowing this, we have already entered more deeply into knowingness.

The inquiry that follows proceeds by way of language and illustrations, and in this sense it is sharply limited. Yet even within these limits, so many kinds of knowledge are available! We are free to speculate and reflect, to visualize and think. We are all familiar with time, space, and knowledge, and we all have our own perspective, our own field of vision. We can go in any direction and explore any dimension. We can play the game in any way we like.

We start from a first-level understanding. But the more we can open to space, the more knowledge can communicate with time, the more readily a second-level openness begins to operate. A sign that this is so may be the realization that space and time cannot be separated, that they are bound to one another, and that the knowledge that lets us identify this particular time and space grows out of this union.

As knowledge deepens into space and time, it touches the first baseline of thought. Then the point-being of time can change, opening space and the objects that appear in space. This dynamic feeds back to the 'I am here'. It reveals 'here' as the thought, the perception, the position, and the interpretation.

At this point knowledge can ask questions that would not make sense earlier, questions that point toward a third level. Are there really only three dimensions of space? Is time confined to past and present and future? How does existence emerge out of nothing? Where do time and space and knowledge meet?

Throughout history, human beings have sensed a dimension to experience that their knowledge cannot grasp, a 'secret' understanding that many traditions call sacred. But that dimension must also be open to knowledge, space, and time. It may be secret, but it is not beyond the range of inquiry.

THE GIFT OF KNOWLEDGE

If knowledge can unite with space and time, the benefits for our time and our world could be significant. Space seems naturally to be healing, letting the tension of restriction melt away. Time brings new vitality, richness, and beauty. And knowledge changes our orientation to our own lives, revealing what we need to know.

These changes first develop 'here'. But once our 'here' has been restored to health, we can extend the benefits 'there' as well. It might be the 'there' of other human beings that we benefit, or the 'there' of our surrounding world, or even the 'there' of our own senses, or of other parts of our lives from which we have somehow become cut off. However it manifests, such a union of 'here' and 'there' is sure to bring a greater sense of harmony and peace, a gentle texture to experience—loving, soft, and welcoming.

The path toward such fundamental change proceeds step by step. Reading what is presented here may be an inspiration to take the first step, and that may be enough. Space will accommodate our efforts, and time will transform all obstacles. We all have the knowledge that will let us begin. There is no reason to delay.

Space

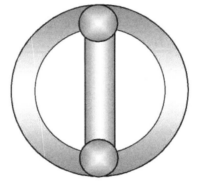

Geometry of a
Living Universe

Whatever our theories, whatever values we hold dear, one thing strikes us as certain: I am here. This conviction creates a frame for everything we experience. It determines our sense of space, our positioning in time, and our identity as knower. Whatever other changes we go through in life, this fundamental triangulation of time, space, and knowledge does not shift. And once this foundation is established, the 'ratios' of conventional knowledge—'this' to 'that', 'now' to 'then', 'here' to 'there'—give us the reference points with which to construct a knowable world.

From any ordinary perspective, questioning the 'I am here' makes little sense. But what have we been able to build on the basis of this foundation? Whether we look at the sweep of the history or at our contemporary world, the record of human achievement is far from perfect. Despite stunning technological achievements and enduring monuments to the human spirit in every civilization, the fact remains that human beings are often unhappy and frustrated, that conflict among individuals and peoples is always with us, and that we still have no real answer to the fundamentals of old age, sickness, and death.

Is there a linkage here? What if all the particularities of our personal lives, all the proclamations and posturings of the great civilizations, all our hopes and aspirations for the future are shaped by the same 'I am here' framework? Does the 'I am here' guarantee that we will take the same perspective, make the same mistakes, encounter the same obstacles?

Suppose this to be so. Suppose it to be even *partially* so. In that case, exploring this 'self-evident' frame of reference may be the most important inquiry anyone can undertake.

Suppose that in accepting the 'I am here' at face value, we limit the ways time, space, and knowledge can operate. We would be drastically reducing our own potential. Yet having accepted such limitations as the truth of our human condition, we would not even see our limits as limits. There would be no room for questioning, no way to frame alternatives.

Do we want to see more than 'I am here' allows? Are we willing to try another way? The basic shapes and structures of our known world are so solid, so self-evident! Could we try something different? Explore other shapes and forms? Let our wonderings unfold without concern for what we know to be so? Suspend our beliefs and certainties?

BEYOND LIMITS

Our conventional understanding offers one view of time, space, and knowledge, a first-level take on our human conditions. But 'beneath' that view, we have access to our concrete embodiment here and now, and that provides a different foundation for inquiry. We are free to pose alternatives, to start over. We are free to refer new theories and new forms of understanding back to direct experience.

'I am here' can be the starting point for countless questions. What does it mean to be here? What does it mean to be? What is the nature of 'here', and how do we come to inhabit the 'here'? If we are 'here', what else is 'there'? Perhaps our immediate presence, our 'here-ness,' could mean many different things.

STARTING WITH HERE

The 'I am here' tells us that existence appears to be somehow related to location. 'Here' creates a sense of closeness in comparison to everything else, which is 'there'. These two points, 'here' and 'there', depend on each other. 'Here' makes no sense without a 'there'.

'There' provides a second point of reference. Now I can go from 'here' to 'there'. At this point we have introduced the idea of movement. There is a going 'from' and 'to'—perhaps physical movement in space, or the movement outward of the senses to the sense object, or the movement of the mind, which governs and interprets the whole.

In this way, a relationship is established. The subject is 'here' and the object 'there'; the subject is 'from' and the object is 'to'.

The structures of 'from' and 'to' apply to space, to time, and to knowledge. But in every realm, they share in a fundamental mystery. If I travel 'to' there, 'there' becomes 'here'. 'Here' has traveled with me, and I am ready for a completely different 'from'. Somewhat surprisingly, while I am certain that everyone has this same experience, when 'I' meet 'you', 'here' remains 'here', while you are quite definitely 'there'.

With 'I am here' the basic structures for time-space-knowledge interactions are in place: the knower in one location, the known object in another, somehow linked to the first, and movement between them. As we observe and question more closely, we can determine with greater precision how time and space work together within this structure, establishing the foundation for knowledge.

It might be easy at this point to chart the ways the known world develops. The knower is the self, and the self identifies a world and objects that have specific characteristics. With this foundation, ordinary reality readily emerges. But we want to proceed differently. Let us stay as close to the fundamental structures as we can. Let us see what alternatives they suggest.

BASELINE

As I move from here to there, I traverse a distance. The shortest distance will be a straight line, a baseline that connects the two points that locate the subject and the object. My sense of 'here' is secured at both the subject and the object poles of the baseline, giving the knowledge, 'I am here'.

Since the 'I am here' comes into being through movement along the baseline, it depends on both space and time. Subject, baseline, and object form an interdependent unit of existence, brought into being by a movement in time through space. Symbolically, we could say that the word 'I' represents this unit: a straight baseline joining the poles of subject and object.

What is the purpose of specifying the baseline? 'From' and 'to' seem sufficient to locate where I am and what I am doing, and we know without the baseline that every 'here' has its 'there'. But that is the point! 'Here' and 'there' are already aligned, joined from the outset. In drawing the line, we articulate the structure that is implicit. Now we can draw forth the implications. We can discover the shape of the 'I am here'.

SUSTAINING AXES

Still, something is missing. I establish 'here' in relation to 'there', but how can either 'here' or 'there' be positioned at a particular location? Here and there go everywhere together, but we might find them anywhere. They are like young children on a trip, never really knowing where they are located, just knowing that they are with their family. To overcome this lack of specificity, the baseline needs endpoints. Otherwise it will continue on endlessly, and there will be no establishing, no particular 'here' and no 'there' after all.

To specify the endpoints, something must 'cut' the baseline and make a mark. To mark a point, we use two lines. In this case, let us use two 'baseline units', one crossing the other at a right angle, defining the location of 'here' as the zero-point, the place in two dimensions where the x-axis and y-axis meet.

POINT OF ORIGIN

The zero-point is the point of origin: the 'from' that makes it possible to establish. But how can the point of origin originate? What is the source of zero?

In mathematics, this would be an odd question. Why should zero, which is nothing, need a source? But that way of putting the question is misleading. It seems self-evident that zero is nothing at all, but we forget that any number is nothing at all. Numbers do not refer to anything real, and so we are free to manufacture them at will. Similarly, zero as a mathematical point has no dimensions. But in our own lives, every point— even the zero-point—enters time and space and comes from time and space, and so it seems fair to say that a certain dimensionality must be at work.

How do we reply to the question of the source of zero? We might just say that the point of origin has no origin; that it emerges from nowhere, like the universe starting up without preconditions from the Big Bang. Unfortunately, this answer shuts down inquiry before it ever has a chance to begin. It also seems to go against common sense. Whatever operates in the world by producing an effect must somehow appear and be active in the world. But how can the point of origin appear, if not on the basis of previous appearances?

Then what is the nature of these previous appearances? The zero-point emerged as zero when we crossed two baselines. Following this lead, we see that the zero-point cannot emerge from one direction only. If a point emerged along just one line, how could it ever emerge; how could it differentiate itself or be 'locatable' as its own unique entity? Instead, a point will have at least two lines of direction or two movements at work in its appearing, like the two 'baseline units' we posited above.

Now, each of those lines of direction must take form as well. A line is called into being by connecting two points, so the emerging of zero at the juncture of two axes requires four points in all. And these points in turn will require four points before they can emerge, giving sixteen points. For our purposes, we can stop with this structure of sixteen, but in fact it seems that the background required for even one zero-point to emerge is infinite in its interactions.

We can arrive at the fullness of sixteen through a slightly different route. The axes that locate zero have four endpoints in all. Each of these endpoints will need its own defining axes, which require four additional endpoints for each point. Again, we have sixteen points in all.

It is interesting to see that once we locate zero on its axes, we become aware that zero itself points in four directions, or has four sides. We might say that zero can allow for sixteen directions, points that we could mark out on its circumference and note as potential directions for movement. It is as though we had found sixteen different 'heres' within the 'here'.

Images of Wholeness

At this point, we can let the nature of our inquiry shift. 'Here' and 'there' have given us certain forms: shapes that reveal and depend on the dynamic of time and the allowing of space. Now we can let those forms suggest further possibilities, informing our investigation. It is almost as if space has been given a voice. Attuned to its presence, we make ourselves at home, waiting to hear what it has to say.

In mathematics, the zero-point where the x- and y-axis meet has no dimensions. It seems unlikely, however, that the 'I am here' would agree to being reduced to non-dimensionality in this way. Since our aim is not precise measurement, let us imagine that the zero-point truly has the two-dimensionality of the symbol 'zero': a circle without substance. We might think of this unexpected dimensionality as the baseline curving back on itself, with the fullness of zero suggesting how the 'here' affirms its own being through the feedback it receives from its interaction with the 'there'. As the 'I' served as our symbol for the 'baseline unit', we could let the curve in the '6' of 16 serve as a symbol for this curving back. Perhaps the same curve can evoke the gravity of appearance, or the curve of time as it sweeps within its dynamic the linear segments of past, present, and future.

MORE DIMENSIONS

In the picture that has developed until now, we have imagined that the lines that indicate the source of zero are somehow 'behind' it. But this seems unduly restrictive. It seems more accurate to imagine them converging on the zero in all directions. In that case, the zero must be three-dimensional: a sphere rather than a circle. Perhaps we could seek permission for this unexpected expansion from our friend, the '6' of 16, which opens to three dimensions by adding to the four primary directions of the compass the orientations up and down.

Once we have conceived of zero as a sphere, we have another way of arriving at 16, for taking the eight points of the compass and repeating them in the third dimension will give us 16 points in all. Rotating through these points will repeat the sphere of our three-dimensional zero (which could also be divided into sixteen sectors).

However, this approach may be too closely bound to the two-dimensional figure with which we began. If we recall that space itself allows all possible forms to appear, we can surely be more adventurous. Let us twist the sphere of zero in half, creating two spheres that suggest the 'here/there' duality. If we halve each sphere again, we have four spheres in the four directions. Following our initial model, we soon arrive again at 16—inherent now in the form of the zero-point sphere.

We should also recall that we are reflecting on the origin of the origin, something that does not 'exist' in any ordinary terms. To suggest this element, we might say that the origin of the origin is located in a fourth dimension. Imagining the 'cube' that would enclose such a four-dimensional space, we arrive at a figure that once again is defined by sixteen points.

Cone of Possibilities

T he fullness of 16 that zero has evoked can also unfold along the baseline. We could imagine a cone with 16 rings, radiating out from the point as its apex. The cone suggests that the zero-point expands in time as well as space, revealing the dynamic inherent in the original 'from' and 'to'.

Since each point that unfolds in the structuring of 16 has the same structure as the zero-point itself, we could identify a cone emerging from each of these points as well; in fact, we could imagine sixteen cones radiating from each of these points, with the open face of each cone another potential zero-point, from which sixteen more cones can emerge. Cone feeds into cone, creating a structure that informs appearance, revealing complexity within even the most simple forms.

As cones expand into more cones, the territory of our known world takes form. But we can choose not to become involved in the specifics of what arises in this way. Instead, we can continue to look more to structure than to form.

If the radiating cone is seen as space accommodating time, or as the momentum of time unfolding space, this raises new questions. Does space increase over time, as the cone expands? Do more objects or interconnections form as the time dimension of the cone lengthens, or as cones give rise to cones in increasing levels of complexity? How does knowledge enter the cone, and how does it make sense of it?

PRECISION AND SPECIFICITY

A good way of exploring such interacting complexities is to turn to the human body. In *Time, Space, and Knowledge* (Berkeley: Dharma Publishing, 1977), conventional appearance is investigated through a series of exercises that focus on visualizing a giant body. The observer is invited to enter the interior of the body through the pores of the skin and proceed to the body's inner recesses. Here, among the organs, tissue, and fluids, the observer can begin to appreciate how each component stands in relation to the space 'between' and 'around'. At the heart of these interconnections is the pulsing aliveness of our own embodiment. Key questions begin to emerge: How does the body as a living organism come into being at all? How do its systems sustain themselves? How are its astonishing variety of shapes, forms, and functions developed and coordinated? How does it all work?

If we 'sink into' these questions deeply, we might see the precision and specificity of our own bodies as resulting from the intersection or convergence of multi-dimensional cones, each a dynamic expression of 16. Tracing out such points of convergence, we find ever finer points, manifesting at multiple levels simultaneously. As the structure of multiple cones becomes more clear, the body, its aliveness, and its functions can all be seen as instances of space-time development: translucent points of being held together by the 'glue' of space.

Symbolic Structuring

In what realm do the structures of directionality and origin operate? They seem to belong to space and time about equally. But they also relate to knowledge. For anything to be known by the mind, it must be a potential point of knowledge, which means that it must be locatable. In turn, this seems to depend on being able to locate in a context that can function as the defining background.

In that case, should the lines of directionality that locate the zero-point be understood as wholly imaginary constructs of the knowing mind? It may be better not to take a stand. If we leave these lines undefined, their very attribute of being wholly open and yet defining may point toward something deeply significant about the realms of time, space, and knowledge. Because they are prior to the system that the zero-point initiates, the defining lines could be said to have an infinite capacity, akin to space itself. And the very concept of a zero point suggests that this quality of openness and indeterminacy, of allowing anything at all, may be carried over into the point of origin that operates at the base or beginning of all we know. In any case, what could constitute the lines, if not more zero-points?

In this description, we do not have to assign a direct role to mind at all. Instead, it may serve us best as a compelling analogy. The mind is open for anything, ready to receive all content. Is the openness of space, as symbolized in the 16 and also in the zero-point, akin to this openness of mind? Is it different?

Magical Body
of Space

What do we learn from these exercises and visualizations? The images we are exploring have no substance in any ordinary sense, but their availability for inquiry does suggest a way of exploring space and time. The baseline gives one dimension, so that is a beginning. The axes give two dimensions, and locating the axes gives three dimensions. Without having specified or measured anything to which we could assign substance, we have already seen a structure unfold in which the zero-point gives rise to sixteen points.

How interesting that 'from' and 'to' immediately generate such complex structures! Once I understand how 'here' and 'there', 'from' and 'to' must function, shape seems to lead to form almost spontaneously, through an inner space dynamic. Perhaps that same dynamic actually operates in space as we know it: from the smallest, most minute particles to the largest structures of the cosmos.

Of course, the image of a zero-point unfolding in sixteen directions cannot readily serve as a model for the way that substance appears. Instead, we might call it a vision. As a vision, it offers a way of seeing that stands in contrast to our usual understanding of what is so.

Why would we want to employ such a vision? Because our ordinary way of seeing leaves out of account all that is most vital in appearance. Wherever we look, we can see that the world is intensely alive. Space is not stagnant, and time is not dead. Whatever beliefs we may hold, we cannot deny the pattern, order, and creativity of the living universe. The power of a volcano, the delicacy of an iris petal, the flashes of human compassion and clarity that appear when least expected— each of these illustrates the remarkable range of phenomena that occurs once we have 'something' rather than 'nothing'. Somehow the 'aliveness' of the universe has found a means of appearing, of taking shape, even of mirroring us back to ourselves.

How is all this possible? In some very real sense, it is a mystery. But in another sense, we are surrounded by the precision and specificity that give an answer. The immediacy of the phenomenal world is always available, unfolding as time, space, and knowledge. Appearance and experience speak to us in a language that is sharp and clear, yet somehow always indecipherable. If we listen closely, exercising our intelligence and imagination, we may begin to understand what is being said. We may sense that the order and beauty of the manifest world are not randomly generated, but point to a deeper order—the magical body of space.

It would hardly be possible to investigate the whole of this magical body in all its specificity. But if our own manifestation 'here' and 'now' is a part of this body; if our own way of existing actually points toward its most fundamental structures, then the inner truth of 'I am here' can become the gateway to deeper knowledge and genuine openness.

FOUNDING POINT OF ACCESS

Let us consider one such possible point of access. As zero expands in all directions and all dimensions, it still remains zero. As the zero gives rise to 16, the 16 remains zero as well. But if zero remains zero, how can it found existence? Perhaps the question is puzzling because we understand existence in terms of substance. The space-time centered knowledge we have been investigating suggests we think instead in terms of motion and location. Once the point marks out 'here', the 'I' as knower, the object, and the linking baseline can all be activated. The 'I am here' can come into operation, and self and world can be built up. But none of these moves departs in any way from zero.

Put differently, we could say that 'I am here' builds only on the basis of space, time, and knowledge, which make available the structures of zero and 16 freely, erecting no walls and establishing no separations. Each point as zero expresses space, and each baseline and each set of axes represents time's potential for dynamic movement. Knowing appearance at this level, knowledge gathers and interprets, structuring what zero gives—setting up the world.

Symbol of Appearance

At the fundamental level, space seems open by nature. It does not develop; it does not have to be modernized or renovated; it does not have to be opened like a frontier. How could there possibly be limits to space? To say that space has a border is to ask what is on the other side of the border. If the answer is "more space," space does not have a border after all, only some kind of barrier whose special qualities would have to be investigated. If the answer is that something solid seals off space, would that solid something not need space in which to appear?

The zero-point shares in the openness of space; it could even be considered a localized (or locatable) symbol of that openness. Suppose I start with a tile mosaic and expand it, until I no longer see the subject of the mosaic, but only the individual colored tiles. If I keep on expanding, the tiles also disappear, and I encounter rough surfaces. Continuing in this way, I come to chains of molecules. Eventually, I reach a realm so empty, so devoid of matter, that I can truly say nothing is there. But even with this 'nothing' I may not have reached the zero-point, where no properties operate, where openness manifests without establishing.

Is zero truly the representative of space? In one sense, it seems strange to make this claim. Why should space 'appear' at all, whether in its own right or through a representative? Perhaps, however, space has its own way of appearing—a way that is closer to symbol than substance. Perhaps zero is such a symbol.

WHOLENESS OF 16

We have seen that zero gives rise to 16. If zero is the point *before* it manifests as point, 16 identifies the precise, exacting means through which zero, having given location, makes possible the move from 'nothing' to structure and form. 16 is the transition of zero, the foundation for the architecture of manifestation.

Even if we suppose that the 'prior' of existence is unknowable, once manifestation is in motion, the symbol of 16 allows us to track its activity. 16 suggests the power of space to locate and allow: the invisible properties, the secret charge, the sacred dimensions.

When we envision cones unfolding in all directions, we see that 16 points back toward the open of zero and forward to the infinite interconnections that link one point to all points. With 16 in operation, no 'fragment' of time, no 'region' of space, no 'version' of knowledge has a completely separate mode of being; each refracts and contains all that exists. Time, space, and knowledge exhibit spontaneously as simultaneity, interpenetration, and knowingness, freed from the restrictions of 'here/there', 'now/then', and 'subject/object'. In all its manifestations, in every instant of the whole, the magical body of space has 16 points.

16 is the abstraction that becomes the fact. Its precision suggests that distinctions can be made, certainty can be reached, actions can be decided. At each point of transition, 16 cones radiate outward, each giving 16 more: the finest divisions, the most refined distinctions. Through the power of 16, pattern, structure, and rhythm are possible.

SHEER DISCERNMENT

Whatever the characteristics or activities we may ascribe to it, 16 could not be a thing. Perhaps we could say it is what makes things go, transmitting and sustaining the aliveness of time-space-knowledge as they shape, allow, and specify. If we imagine that appearance passes into being through the gate of 16, then from a first-level knowledge perspective, 16 is a sacred, secret code. Never fully decipherable, it always holds out the key that will reveal its meaning.

Between zero-point and existence, the convergence of the whole somehow arises. 16 marks that point, the point where the compass can construct. It is the point of transition and the transition of the point. It is the unification of the field, the gathering point of time, space, and knowledge.

Manifestation
of Form

At one level, form can be expressed through the geometry of interacting shapes and symbolic numbers. But the world of form is a world of creation and dissolution, expansion and contraction, connections and transitions. The being-point takes countless forms.

Whenever we examine or experience any structure, we are in some way involved in understanding how its various parts relate to one another. At the heart of this relation-making is the ratio, a mechanism for understanding how this world of strongly specific interactions can evolve from points and 16.

For instance, in listening to a piece of music, we discern various relationships of tone, rhythm, melody, tempo, and texture. Liking or disliking the music is in large measure a statement about how we perceive the relationships that make up the whole.

Similarly, when we enter a well-designed house, we experience various qualities rooted in the relationships of form, space, color, movement, and light. Even when we are not consciously aware of these reactions, our response to being in the house springs from a very quick and efficient 'sizing up' of the relationship of different parts to one another, and ultimately to the whole of the structure.

Suppose we left the house and passed through its yard into the streets of the town. We would now be perceiving a new and wider array of relationships: the relationship of house to house, block to block, and so on. As we reached the edge of the town, we would move on to yet wider relationships: town to countryside, countryside to seashore, continent to continent.

There is no pre-established limit to the scope of such an investigation, whether we move out into the larger universe or explore the complexity of the microscopic and subatomic realms. Whether we examine a water molecule, a work of abstract art, or a supernova, certain underlying principles apply. These principles include the perception of difference, distinction, order, structure, and scale, all directly experienced as a certain living and dynamic quality that gives rise at another level to our judgments of like and dislike.

Ratio could be considered as these relationships, expressed in their most fundamental form. Far more than a numerical relationship, such as 2/3, ratio seems connected to the implicit structuring that pervades the world, including our perception of that world. Without the underlying perception of ratio, our experience would be like thick pea soup: no distinction, no precision, no clear form.

To draw a single line, we need the equation of the ratio (for instance, the ratio of 'here' to 'there'); to determine and distinguish, we need the ratios of sameness to difference. But the mind that determines is also the outcome of ratio, and the knowledge that differentiates stands in a ratio to the knowledge of the whole. Time's directionalities are ratios, and the boundaries in space that arise through measurement are ratios as well. Each exclusion manifests a ratio, and each intimacy also.

How do we discern the distinctions that trace back to the ratio? How are we able to perceive difference? Why is the phenomenal world around us sharp and alive, rather than vague and hazy? Perhaps we can take a clue from observing that any kind of distinction—between one 'thing' and another, one thought and another, one experience and another—implies space, which allows the difference to manifest, and time, which empowers change.

DYNAMICS OF APPEARANCE

The more we explore ratio, the more we see its living, dynamic quality. For instance, in the relation between the trunk, a branch, and a leaf of a tree, each has relative independence, but each is linked to the others. The tree itself is in a living ratio with the earth it springs from, as well as the earth and air it transforms into. In the same way, the body has its own living ratio of relationships, both internal and external. In one sense there is a boundary—between root and soil, or flesh and oxygen; in another sense the ratio helps make clear that boundaries and edges are as much connecting points as they are dividing lines.

How does ratio articulate change and transition, for instance, from 'before' to 'after'? It seems that it must engage the structuring of difference in space and time. Seen in this way, ratio is already active within 16, differentiating as arising takes form.

Perhaps more fundamentally, when 16 reaches completion, ratio is what sets manifestation in motion, making transition possible. Through the ratio, matter can move, perceptions can reach reality, and thoughts can evoke. Even in the distances of interstellar space, where galaxies move in solemn splendor, ratio determines and engages.

From our perspective, inhabiting a world that has taken form, space and time both have living ratios to what appears and unfolds. Time conducts the ratio, making visible the sense of 'was' and 'is' and 'will be', feeding appearance into space. In a sense it is ratio that 'connects' space and time as well, holding appearance together in the absence of boundaries.

For our embodied existence, the ratio makes real, inviting fulfillment. But ratio also unfolds into the final transition of death. At that moment there are no extensions. If we imagine looking back from the moment of death, what we might see is the ratio of opportunity to actual participation.

KNOWLEDGE OF RATIO

R atio gives distinction without discrimination or hierarchy. Like a tape measure, the ratio is neutral. Lower knowledge turns ratio into judgments, narrowing, and excluding, but that is not the inherent structure of ratio at all. To judge is to turn from the openness of ratio to the arrogance of the pre-established.

Knowledge attuned to the significance of the ratio proceeds quite differently. It sees in ratio the boundless creativity that marks the ongoing transition from openness to form. Through ratio, it celebrates space allowing as the heart of appearance.

Such a second-level knowledge penetrates the shadows that fall when pre-determined points fill up the openness of space. Reveling in diversity, it recognizes the ratio as the perfect manifestation of space. Knowing how to operate the ratio, knowledge can make its point without being bound by it. It can choose how to act and determine the controlling structure. We might consider such knowledge of the ratio as itself the ratio of first to second-level knowledge.

RATIOS OF THE WHOLE

W e could imagine that at the zero, being is so open that time and space do not act. It is as if the zero slept, 'doing' nothing and 'informing' nothing.

Change comes with the ratio. The ratio activates zero and engages the completion of 16, allowing the universe established through form in space and action in time to take birth. In this sense, every 16 is a ratio brought to fullness, a transition of the whole.

Without the ratio to give specifics, every point is zero, and every point engages 16 dimensions of time, space, and knowledge. With everything in transition, nothing is established. With the ratio, a very subtle shift occurs. 16 zero-points unfold together, manifesting limit, form, and meaning. The eye of the frog develops; a particular density engages; a gravitational field exerts more pull; a casual thought leads toward a specific fantasy.

From the perspective of ratio, none of this can happen without a 'prior'. In this way of seeing, 16 has an inner structure, a sequencing from one to 15. Before 16, all is undecided. Will the point manifest? What form will it take? Will the opportunity pass by unheeded, suddenly catapulted into the realm of the impossible?

Along the axes that establish the point, a dynamic hovers between positive and negative, between taking form and going unrealized. At 15 the whole is available, but the clarity that will lead to the final determination is still lacking. The background has not crystallized.

At 16 all this changes. The 'right' ratio forms, the pool of possibilities takes hold as a precise form and specific design. A definitive kind of wholeness coheres. The dynamic of locating reaches the necessary intensity, allowing for specificity, quality, and character, for the ability to move and change, for 'to-be' and 'not-to-be'.

HIDDEN HARMONY

P erhaps each step in the sequence that unfolds from 1 to 15 has its own 16: 16 opening into 16 opening into 16 and so on. If so, we could imagine that the sequence can be interrupted; that the ratio guiding these transitions does not hold. When the 16 of the whole does cohere, perhaps a further ratio is required: a point of juncture between 16s, a juxtaposition necessary for form to take place. Perhaps there are other complexities as well, unknown to us, or even unthinkable.

From this perspective, looking backward from the ratio, we may marvel that anything takes form at all. For space and time, however, there is no mystery, for there is no difficulty and no piling up of improbabilities. As the plant unfolds from the seed, so space allows and time discloses.

We might think of all this as happening in a fourth dimension, where time and space and knowledge have always met and will always be available to one another. In that dimension (which is neither 'here' nor 'there'), the ratio of what is has already taken form, the location has already been determined. There is interaction without possibility of interference or obstruction, of being excluded or going astray.

Space
Performance

In the common-sense view, space surrounds existent bodies and is also within them. Even where matter is present, it occupies space and depends on space. Without space, there would be nothing to talk about, nothing to be known. Space is the 'prior' of existence. If it were not available as matter's 'other', matter in its essence could not come to be.

The same does not seem true for space. We can at least conceive of totally empty space, devoid of matter. In that case, what is the 'other' or the 'prior' for space? What establishes it? Or must it remain unestablished?

Space as the background invites existence, but that is not all. It also accommodates the coordination of sense experience, the interconnection of objects, the substantiality of what exists, and the unifying of all physical appearance within a single matrix. Each of these operations or capacities is independent, yet somehow space can perform them all.

Finally, for something to be present in space, we ourselves must be present to what is presented. How does something become present for us? If we do not have a category among our mental constructs that will take it in, can it appear at all? What does this question suggest about the relationship between mind and space? Even if we are not philosophers, answers to this question pop up almost immediately. But can we just look, without presuppositions?

KNOWLEDGE IN SPACE

Mind is the background for cognition, the root of sensory experience. Since such experience is what allows us to structure out the existence of particular things, we might say that mind and space are partners, equally operating existence as we know it. In that case, what is the relation between mind and space? For instance, unless mind had available the idea of 'space', could we make any sense of existence at all? What about ideas such as 'the universe' or 'the visual field'? How much can we simplify our mental framework and still maintain awareness of the world? How strongly do we depend on the *concept* of space in constituting our world, or even in deciding what it means to constitute?

We think of space as somehow physical (even though it does not exist!). Yet the 'operators' that let us make sense of space—'from' and 'to', distance and separation—depend on our knowing capacity. Knowledge (as capacity rather than content) responds to what appears, but it is also responsible for its appearance. We ourselves are knowledgeable, and the world we know is knowledgeable as well, at least in allowing itself to be known.

The knowables of a knowledgeable world emerge into being in a way that is sharp and clear, which means that time presents them as available. We could imagine a time that was somehow impenetrable to knowledge, dead and diffuse, but that is not the way it is. In that case, what can we say of the relationship of space to time? Can we understand space as 'within' time, in the sense that the whole of space 'exists' right now? If space does not exist, we might imagine that it is timeless. But in that case, how can we account for the ability of space to allow an existence that unfolds through past, present, future?

Giving Form

I f space did not operate or allow, time would have to be a property of appearance. But space and time seem inextricably linked and universally available. Whatever appears appears in both space and time simultaneously. And whatever appears to us is known by knowledge. This triple interaction of time-space-knowledge is also the juncture of our human being: the fundamental that shapes who we are.

Looking in time and space, we see the patterns and dynamics of consequences; engaging what appears in time and space, we act as human beings. Taking and responding, accepting and rejecting, we act into time, space, and knowledge. It seems that the choices we make are reflected in their interplay.

At the same time, we are part of the universe. But the universe itself 'takes form': Time gives birth, knowledge exhibits, space allows. Where does this creativity manifest? How does it develop? What is its 'from' and 'to'?

As we act into this unfolding, do we have any choice? How can we draw shape and form from the universe? Are we the ones with the power to shape time and space, or is it someone else? What role do we play?

Finally, can we trace out in the operations of space-time-knowledge some understanding of our human destiny? How does one work out one's destiny? In what arena? Do we move toward our destiny in linear sequence? Does guiding vision unfold in linear time and physical space at all?

No Occupancy

In conventional terms, we could identify two kinds of space: occupied and unoccupied. Unoccupied space could be considered pure potentiality, undefined and indiscernible, pregnant with all possibilities.

Is there also a third kind of space, still more purely available, before form has been conceived or entered the space womb? For instance, before we were born, where was the space that our body now occupies? Before we had our first thought, where was the space in which the mind conducts its operations? Where will such space go after we die? When the body dies, we can burn it on a funeral pyre, but where is the fire that would singe the openness of space?

With the occupancy of space, points emerge. Yet when space is occupied by form, it must retain its essential characteristics of openness and allowingness; otherwise, it would not be space, and existence could not arise.

Could there be a point that occupied the whole of space? If points arise in being located, the answer seems to be no—such a cosmic point would be inseparable from space itself. In that case, every point has neighbors.

Each point moves toward 16, but each equally draws on the allowingness of space, the openness of the zero. Then do points share space with one another? Is the 16 of one point connected with the 16 of its neighbor? Is the structure of such sharing the founding mechanism that makes possible the arising of shape and form?

With each point come junctures that can be new starts, new beginnings. The point arrives ready to move out along the baseline, to move toward the completion of 16, to move within the dimensions of time. But movement is not necessarily linear. Perhaps the baseline of any point curves; perhaps such curvature is necessary so that complex, multidimensional forms can emerge, delineated by interconnected points that constitute the defining lines. Perhaps that is why we can speak of the 16 points within each point, capable of opening into cones segmented into rings. Perhaps that is why we can say that the ratio operates and informs.

Structure
of Zero

How can space serve as a cause? How can it even allow? In genuine openness, there is not even zero. If we imagine zero 'in' space, hanging there like a balloon, we have almost certainly gotten it wrong. Then how can we say that zero is the symbol of space?

If we focus on the shape of zero, we find a line in the shape of a circle, a curving edge that connects only to itself. Inside the line is space, and outside the line is space: the edge is the edge between space and space, and so it is not an edge at all. This 'edge that is no edge' is the fitting symbol of space.

From that perspective, every line that defines and gives shape is a symbol—space within, space without: an edge without substance. Every line, every shape returns to zero as the symbol of space: every beginning, every ending, even every existent!

We might think of zero as a remark by space, a saying that expresses an allowing. Space shows itself in zero. It marks out as zero the point-being of the point. When space remarks zero, zero is the point, but also the pointer, pointing to all points as space. In authorizing zero, space decertifies all points. Through the single remark of zero, space allows for all of existence.

As the remark of space, zero must translate what has been said, becoming the starting point for innovation. With point and line and 16 and cone, this process is set in motion. The mark becomes the logos, source for measurement, distance, language, and physical phenomena. Space and time unfold into being.

The remark is a mere reflection of space, a comment on space openness. But it founds all appearance. Zero itself is a reflection on space: the space communication of point-being. Having said this, however, we must add that the highest mountain, the deepest ocean, the most powerful star are also space reflections, no different in their essence than the imaginary line separating space within from space without.

ZERO MOMENTUM

Zero as the symbol of space seems able to allow the arising of form in two distinct ways. First, as the edgeless edge, the line that does not divide, it serves as the allowing occasion for all distinctions and every measure. For instance, we find it in the curve of the '6' that we add to one to arrive at 16. We find it in the axes and baseline, and in the defining of the distance that separates 'here' from 'there'.

As the symbol of form, the place-holder, zero speaks in all language and in each connection. As the voice of space, it is knowledge communicating with time and space, making all meanings. Knowledge draws the circle that gives zero shape, and zero in turn communicates what knowledge chooses to shape. Zero makes possible the 'what' of 'where', the form that holds meaning, the moving from point to point.

Second, zero serves as the foundation, the zero-point that is taken over by the 'I am here'. Through the zero-point of 'here', knowledge takes a perspective. Implicit in this first step is all the rest: from 'from', to 'to', to baseline. This is zero as 16, the generating point for countless other points; zero as circumference of the sphere—360 degrees of zero. Each zero-point can hold the line and uphold the form, and each zero can be endlessly divided into other zeros that open into other directions. A zero-momentum unfolds the whole.

SPACE REFLECTION

Looking at every possible zero-point, every manifestation of form, can we say they are? In one sense, the answer is no. Zero is the reflection of space, and this is the source of its bounty. Unlike substance, zero can never be used up. Mathematics confirms it: Any number divided by zero is infinity.

Then can we say that zero is not? This also seems wrong. Within each zero, a powerful dynamic, belonging equally to space and time, manifests directions and dimensions, perspectives and orientations. If we took the smallest unit of matter and divided and divided it, we would never arrive at zero. Yet without zero to manifest and construct, what would there be to divide?

What can we make of this play between 'yes' and 'no', neither one nor the other. Perhaps we could think of two mirror images of mirror images, each reflecting the other. Perhaps we could speak of layers of space, like the pages of a closed book, but each interpenetrating the others. Space reflecting time allows; time reflecting space presents. The moving image makes the point, and the subjective knower, engaging open momentum, sees itself reflected in the world it knows.

When all is reflection, nothing is divided from anything else. All points remain connected in all directions. Time and space go everywhere together: motion that ripples through the whole fabric of being. All is alive with the dynamic of time, all is inseparable with the everywhere of space.

Such a creation seems beyond the power of first-level knowledge to perceive with complete clarity, not because knowledge lacks the power, but because the structures that have been established no longer allow for it. There is nothing here for interpretations, meanings, and rational conclusions. Still, we can find a voice that speaks to this condition. On the one hand, we have the structures of 16 and the cone, of 'from' and 'to', inviting a more open understanding of what we call the 'I am here'. On the other hand, we have speculation, speaking in surprised tones of 'reflection' and of 'layers' of space. When language is most open, space may be most available. Then we can tell the story without expecting too much. We have a way to suggest what is meaningful.

CAN AND MAY

Whatever appears in space also takes time. What is the right story to tell about this interplay? What might time and space have to say?

Since space is free and open and all-allowing, time comes on the scene, making available the 'now' that existence requires. Together, time and space are partners. Space says, "You may!" Time replies, "I can!" With this exchange, creation, development, momentum, and existence can all function freely.

We might imagine space opening the door for time, but this is misleading, for the space door has always been open. We might imagine time awakening space from its sleep, but this is misleading also, for if time's 'can' were not already implicit in space openness, space-allowing would be a broken promise.

For the zero-point to open, time's 'can' is required; for transitions to take hold, time must engage. The openness of space 'can' be developed, and so it is. Time steps in instantly, without regard to past and present and future. There is only 'can' and 'can' and 'can'.

For space to present a point, time must step in; for the point be opened, space must be available. The dynamic of time powers the momentum of the point, its trajectory through conventional space and time, which becomes the foundation for the line, and thus for change and transition. Time presents the 'can' of candidacy, the 'can' of accommodation, and the 'can' of accomplishment, and space allows them all. Derivation and direction arise, giving 'from' and 'to', but time remains free to move in all directions.

CAN AND CANNOT

Knowledge reads the 'can' of time and space and gives it final form. But the order that first-level knowledge discloses reveals more of 'cannot' than of 'can'. Limitations and boundaries seem to hold the upper hand. We cannot extend time, cannot expand space, cannot change patterns or revise habits, cannot open up emotional knots, cannot rearrange the senses. . . . The list goes on. What has become of the power of time and the openness of space in the reality of our lives?

The answer to the puzzle lies in space openness. When the point is open, 'cannot' cannot be, for allowing is complete. But when openness is not available, 'cannot' comes to the fore.

We might think of this in terms of light and dark. When light disappears, is it gone? When light returns, does darkness go somewhere else? Suppose I leave a room and turn off the light. I have created a ratio of darkness, so that the light can no longer manifest. But the light is available: In very practical terms, the grid that supplies the energy to the electrical wiring remains in place. In contrast, when I turn on the light, the circuit is full: No special ratio needs to be activated.

In lower-level terms, we would speak of the point of balance between positive and negative as lying between the two. But when we look in terms of space openness, the true point of balance comes in the fullness of the positive, in the priority of openness and the 'can'. By nature, space has no 'cannot'.

We might also put it very differently. If 'can' is the ruler, 'cannot' serves as its loyal attendant. Through 'cannot' time and knowledge develop restrictions based on perspectives and juxtapositions. Differences and distinctions form, carving up space openness.

This development holds the potential for great elegance and beauty. Together with time, space takes form and gives structure in countless ways. But it is up to knowledge to link such structures to space openness. If knowledge cannot open to space, the 'can' is swallowed up by 'cannot'. That is the situation we find ourselves in.

When knowledge keeps space openness available, 'can' is everywhere. Space can, time, can, knowledge can. Alternatives present themselves in profusion. Everything is possible. We can do it too—whatever we want, however we wish to. The 'yes!' of time and the 'yes!' of space open all potential. This is the reality of time and space together.

Depth of Zero

I f zero were nothing, it could play no role at all. But even though zero cannot be said to exist, it is always linked to location, and location is not nothing. Wherever location operates, the zero-point is active.

As the localization of space, zero has no edge or boundary. Conventional knowledge assigns it a shape, for the shapes and forms that space carves out of time are what conventional knowledge knows. But that is not what zero is about at all.

The appearance of zero seems guided by depth. Like an onion that can be peeled and peeled away forever, zero keeps going. It opens and allows, opens and allows. Its depth is pure, without specification. Conventional knowledge designates 'here' and 'there', 'up' and 'down', but for the zero-point all directions move toward the center, and all points are connected. As the whole of space, zero remains open for all possibilities: It denies time no opportunities and sets knowledge no limits.

Even when specified as starting point, zero does not abandon this unending depth. 'From' is the same as 'now', and 'here' is not separate from 'there'. There is no need for exclusion, for an 'other' that stands at a distance. Yet that is what we will not accept. When we carve out the distance from 'here' to 'there', we also erect a Great Wall between ourselves and the zero-point. We make our own private time and space.

To build our wall, we need to define a new zero, for we must have a starting point on this side of the wall.

But 'new zero' is 'old zero', whether we acknowledge it or not. The wall may be a barrier for us, but not for zero. For what can we use to build the wall but space and time; how can we construct it except with further 'zero starting points'?

If this is so, zero is always available. The depth of space is here. We can be who we are, knowing this is nothing special. Within our localized structures, beneath our starting point, we can reverse the zero-point.

In this there is nothing mysterious. It is just that we are accustomed to focusing on differences or sameness, and difference and sameness both miss the point. What matters is depth.

In depth we discover connections. Language connects, through sound. The atmosphere connects, through oxygen. The earth connects, by giving life.

Most fundamentally, we connect through space and time. We are here, with everything else; we are now, not separate from all that ever has been and will be. Space and time are not the producers of a play put on for our benefit, and we are not theater-goers who can leave at the end of the performance. In the heart of our being we are bonded to space and time, more surely than water is bonded to wetness.

DIRECTION AND LOCATION

T he power of zero-space finds expression in the lines of direction that give dimensionality. Each dimension opens the depth of zero as the space of location, a structuring that does not depend on the directionality of observation. In the depth of being located, each zero-point has neighbors in each direction. Connection and action are possible. The potential for shape and form is there, available for interaction with the power of time.

The curving of space and the carving out of form do not come to an end, for there is always another direction, and every direction allows existence. In the neighborhood in which we live, there is always more room to build, and always more time to begin construction. Even at the edge of black holes, knowledge pronounces space and time suitable. How could there be space that was out of bounds to existence; that sealed itself off? How could there be a barrier to time's momentum? History and existence have space permission. Nothing holds them back.

Self in Space

Through the openness of space accommodation and the locating power of the zero, points appear. Interacting in space and time, they manifest characteristics, qualities, and division, and discern distinctions between 'from' and 'to'. Their activity encompasses the whole of existence and all experience. Yet in the end, the point stays true to its own point-being, which returns to zero-creativity.

Parented by space and time, the point of being has the potential to know. It carries knowledgeability, just

as a gene carries strands of DNA. The 'here/there' structure of 'I am here' establishes the knower and assigns to
time and space certain rigid properties, but that way of
looking may get it all backwards. Why not let time-
space-knowledge say it differently? Why not acknowledge this trinity as it establishes the point-being, creating
the axes of our being and locating self in space and time.
Would such a saying not give greater freedom? Would
such a meaning touch us differently?

Space
Qualities

S pace embraces all existents in all directions. It circles through 360 degrees of completion: the full circumference of being. Suppose that the patterns of time likewise run in 360-year cycles, transitioning in countless ways from known to unknown to known. How could knowledge not respond? Holding the key and taking the initiative, establishing the purpose and means, knowledge would surely pronounce the names and categories right for each ratio of time and space, demonstrating where to draw the lines and how to draw the benefits.

Unfolding Treasure of Space

T he beauty of the exhibition opened by space far surpasses aesthetics, and the qualities that emerge from space are breathtaking in their nobility and value. They fill our hearts with such richness that we may easily find ourselves in a love affair with space.

Through space openness, mind relaxes, uncrowded by pressured thoughts, and time slows, so that the wonders of zero and 16 can manifest. The knowledge that comprehends space grows, showing us how to cherish space and use its treasures.

Beneath the surface of separate appearances, everything in the universe connects to space, heart to heart. All edges are united by deep lines of space. Imagine the still of night, with everyone asleep; suddenly, through magic, the roof of every house is lifted off—all imagined spaces merge, all the secret thoughts flow into one.

JOURNEY INTO SPACE

Space has endless places for us to explore and enjoy. Guided by knowledge, we can make a great journey into the mysteries of space. Knowledge delights in exercising in wide open spaces: the space of the physical world, the body that embodies space, the space of experiencing life, the space of knowledge itself.

Once we decide to undertake the journey, space and time support our choice. Soon knowledge uncovers wonderment. Space opens, and appreciation for life overflows old boundaries. Head and heart join together, inviting knowledge, and knowledge responds, cherishing the feeling in the heart that makes being love to dance. The journey enters unknown realms, more exciting, more spontaneous, and more nourishing than we had ever imagined.

Touching the wonder of space increases the meaning and purpose of life. Love of knowledge intensifies, and being is understood. Until that omega is reached, knowledge opens and opens. It moves toward 360, toward first and last, alpha and omega—complete being. Zero and the perfection of 16 embrace everything.

The sphere of 360 opening in space allows all being. The shape is carved in space, but the edges are not edges, and no limits can be reached. Every edge of every point opens a gateway into the treasures of space.

FINEST PROTECTION BY SPACE

Space moves within us, and we ourselves move within space. We are always opening to space, and space is always open for us. If we understand this much about space, time manifests differently, with a more allowing rhythm, offering knowledge new points of access. We open to the ratio, to form without edge or character, and discover a rich vitality that is like living forever. We fall in love with space.

To abide in the love of space is the finest of all protections. In love with space, we are surrounded by warmth and wonder that can never be lost, only forgotten. Space is our pervasive partner, closer to our being than any form.

United with space, what transitions could we fear? What ups and downs of time could disrupt our joy?

What hostile territories could we encounter? Space has made treaties with them all, assuring us safe passage.

SPACE TEACHES KNOWLEDGE

In the warm openness of space, learned meanings and imposed purposes give way to spontaneous nourishment. Time's rigid rhythms melt toward fluidity and flexibility, choices abound, and knowledge has ample time to see. Eagerly, thoughts and senses explore what space means. They discover space accommodation, ever endeavoring to open each point.

Secure within the creative space of the heart, incisive knowledge develops easily and rapidly. The point of every point is seen, all part of the appreciation of space. All objects accommodated by space speak up, inviting: "We are here!" All appearance teaches living knowledge.

FEEL OF SPACE

In the house of being embodied, all can become space. Once we enter and abide there, the field-momentum of color, texture, and quality radiate deep vibrancy and warmth—the feel of space coming closer, inviting us, surrounding us on all sides, in all directions. The field fills with light that shines within all color and form.

Nature, art, and music, and all creations everywhere exhibit the beauty of space in an ecstatic play, known in ancient times as lila.

The heart can hardly contain such boundless and intense beauty; the spirit can barely accommodate the richness of touching space directly and incisively. Yet once in the womb of space, united beyond barriers, being relaxes, free of any interference, any possibility of loss. Here is freedom. Here is home.

Time

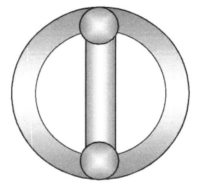

Life Time

Time is time to live, time to grow, and time to die. Time is the partner of space, and their marriage brings forth the whole physical universe, from galaxies and planets to molecules and atoms. We live in time; we experience in time. Time is everywhere actively dynamic in every particle of space.

Yet unless we make a special effort, time itself is almost invisible to us. We notice that the leaves are turning brown, and then the winter snow and rain begin; we admit that we are growing older; we observe changes in our societies; we rush from day to day under the pressure of time's flow. But we do not see the splendid power of time itself.

During our own lifetime, time will present us with abundant moments that pass unappreciated. We walk along the bridge built by these moments, traveling through time—our time. What would we do if we had no moments in which to travel? If no time existed for experience to take place, how could a single atom spin in space? How could the earth's crust fill with oceans that give rise to living forms? How could millions of years of meetings and partings at last create human beings? Surely time is our true ancestor.

Time is our closest friend, our most intimate lover. It flows through our being, beating our hearts, driving our thoughts, moving the breath. Joining the senses with their objects, bridging the gap between subject and object, time charges space with live connections. Time forges networks of creativity that transmit the power to articulate endless shapes and forms. Every corner of space is filled with elegant geometries crafted by time's incredibly synchronized maneuvers. Not an atom is out of place, never a beat is missed.

If we fail to recognize that we belong to time, we do not draw inspiration from the power of time, the way that knowledge does, nor do we delight in the play of time, the way that space does. Immersed in time, do we touch its flow directly? Do we experience the actual dimensionality of time, the dynamic architecture of past, present, and future?

TIME AS HUMAN DESTINY

Master of all changes, time creates and destroys. It opens the doors to the future with one hand and closes the doors to the past with the other. Our role is to follow along the corridors of time, not knowing where they lead. Does this magnificent power have no destiny? Is the display of such wizardry without purpose?

Since we are subject to the regime of time, time's destiny and ours may well be linked. So the entire vector of our own past-present-future becomes meaningful, the history of existence significant, worthy of deep appreciation and exploration. The present becomes an opportunity to fulfill the deepest human yearnings; the future becomes the imminent celebration of our unfolding destiny.

If time belongs to us in the way that we belong to time, then all of history and all the future as well are our frontier, awaiting exploration. Time's creative power is our power too, and we have the ability, the invitation, and the license to investigate the processes of time. Could such an inquiry reveal time's dynamics directly? Could we see the causes and consequences in time's processes as time itself? Could knowledge look into time as its own energy and momentum?

If we thought we had no chance to explore, that we lacked the right or the capacity to inquire into the depths of time, what would our human life become? What would it mean to say that we could not come to know the time that flows through the human embodiment like its heart's blood? Could the human spirit tolerate such alienation?

We say: "I am here." But what does it mean to be in this space and time, with this knowledge? Do we know what our position is as human beings? Such questions, the simplest and most fundamental, are the hardest to ask. Yet if we can frame them clearly and dare to inquire, they have behind them the power of all time, space, and knowledge.

DYNAMIC OF TIME

T ime's dynamic fathers all points, all forms and shapes, all qualities and characteristics. All powers of nature are the power of time—electromagnetic, gravitational, atomic, chemical, biological, and geological. All the forces of history, whether social, political, or economic, derive their power to bring about change from time. Time grows, time develops, time energizes, time brings to life.

The most basic and mysterious force of all, time manifests in movement—changes in position in space, from the subatomic to the intergalactic. Time inspires space to open up dimensionality: Through time's stimulation, depth emerges. Direction and speed, vibration and rotation, all possible moves belong to the magic of motion, and time works its wonders through their changes. Shifting the speed or the direction creates possibilities for new connections and different transitions. By growing one side of a leaf faster than the other, time creates a distinctive shape. By tilting the planet's axis, time makes the seasons progress.

Once motion operates, there is 'from' and 'to', 'before' and 'after'. Everything has its place in time, which is another way of saying that everything does not happen all at once. Events are timed out in sequences.

Without the sequencing of time, one event would not lead to another, and space would be stagnant. There could be no causes and effects, no ordering of any kind, from atomic to psychological.

From our vantage point here in this galaxy and solar system, we cannot trace all causes and effects, but we do comprehend our planet as part of a vast network of natural processes that have developed over long periods of time. Steps and stages can be partly marked out and understood—from the creation of particles to the creation of stars and planets. Certain events precede others, certain events follow in their wake. Time lays out pathways for development, some random, others strongly determined.

When our earth developed to the point where life forms could appear, how many more degrees of complexity were added to time's unfolding? How many processes had to develop to create and operate the first functioning cells? The development of any plant or animal from seed to embryo to adult involves the intricate coordination of varying rhythms of growth. Every level of organization must be coordinated to all the others—from atomic particles and biochemical molecules to geological processes determining the environment of the oceans where the first cells arose.

When we consider the range of human history, we encounter further levels of interconnection, starting with the rise and fall of civilizations, each with its own life span, rhythms, and radius of influence. All our human disciplines—philosophy, religion, art, medicine, psychology, government, economics—find varying expression at different times in history. Ideas fertilize one another, techniques and tools inspire one another, theories war with each other. Decisions in one realm proliferate to other realms. Timing is crucial: If a few key events had taken place at different times, whole lines of development would be transformed.

In any realm we investigate, we see endless variations of distinctive and unique forms, expressing rhythmic patterns. Every leaf is different from all others, every cat is different from all others. At the same time, time elaborates specific themes. Similarities based on group patterning appear, as do symmetries, reflections, and reiterations. These patterns can be perceived as rhythms in space and time, some of the most easily recognizable being in music and the cycles of nature. Once a pattern has been established, time's dynamic may generate precise feedback mechanisms, keeping rhythms delicately balanced, or instituting spirals that move upward or downward with profound effects.

Form seems to have expanded through time, filling more and more space. Time opens up space; it lends knowledge its power to proliferate its designs. More objects fill our space today than filled the world of our grandparents. Our societies are producing enormous quantities of things, and the planet's population is increasing. We simply have more history behind us: More books have been printed, more wars have been fought, more events have taken place.

Time's power to create is also the power to uncreate. With the power to connect and unite comes the power to disconnect and disunite, to reconnect and reunite in new ways. Time 'runs out' for a particular form, and it dies; the old geometry disappears and a new one takes its place. Instead of moving outward in expansion, time's power can turn inward, so that stars, societies, and cells collapse in on themselves.

How are all these connections made? How does the sequencing operate? How is one set of sequences coordinated with another, and how do the consequences of one event transmit through time to a later event? How does time unfold beginnings of forms in space, then make them grow or disappear? If we were to condense all of these questions into a single query, perhaps it would be this: How do time's transitions work?

CONSISTENCY AND CHANGEABILITY

Embedded within time like fish within water, we presently live in the temporal domain without deeply exploring its qualities, its dimensions, or its functioning. Is it because we fear its power to bring our personal world to an end that we try our best to ignore time? Yet ignoring time is like ignoring our own life, our very existence.

All of cosmic history is governed by time, and all the human disciplines study the processes revealed in time. We grapple with the unfolding of time, study the events it presents, and catalog and investigate the enormous array of things it manifests. We devote enormous efforts to controlling and manipulating time, often to no avail. Nonetheless, surrounded by all our knowledge of time's manifestations and developments, we do not know the central point—how time itself works.

Today we have more data at our command than ever before. If we want to look back ten thousand years to imagine the time of ancient humans, we know enough to paint a fascinating picture. We might compare that picture to where we are now, marveling at the changes, astounded at how far we have come. We might also consider the strength of the continuity, the unfailing transmission of human qualities and knowledge from generation to generation in an unbroken line. If we look ahead ten thousand years, and imagine a similar magnitude of change and a similar transmission, can we conceive of where the human race will be?

Such an exercise, carried out with real reflection, may help evoke the power of time. But still we fail to recognize time's consistency and its changeability as the marvels they are, worthy of inquiry and wonderment. Not wondering, we do not think to investigate.

Because we do not know the motions, the rhythms, or the transitions of time, we have never solved age-old questions about time's creative mechanisms. We do not know the dynamic that powers human destiny, and our personal beginnings and endings remain a mystery. Nor can we predict the future beyond the most general conditions. We imagine that we are at the crest of the wave of time, the culmination of billions of years of history, the tip on the forward-looking arrow of time. But how can that be when we do not even know where we are headed?

CRITICAL PATH OF KNOWLEDGE IN TIME

Human destiny is human knowledge. Knowledge is the altar at which we worship, our refuge and our support. But throughout the long eras of human history, we have somehow not developed incisive knowledge. Our understanding seems to get easily stuck in limited, repeating circles that tend to spiral downward; our ideas are not uplifting, often not even livable. Patterns of ordinary knowledge simply play themselves out over and over in time. Reduction leads to more reduction, which leads to contradiction, which leads to conflict, which feeds back, creating confusion, which leads to chaos and disorder, which destroy knowledge and the prospects for knowledge.

This downward path of knowledge in time can be traced psychologically, socially, and historically. Relying only on past-based knowledge, imprinting old answers, we can only repeat the past. We run in vicious circles, reaping more consequences that keep us oriented in the same direction. Without thoroughly understanding our own actions, how can we help but deepen the grooves that limited knowledge is making in time?

If we do not inquire into how these limits and this not-understanding are established and how they flourish, we shall surely suffer from the consequences. The circles of experience will grow tighter and tighter, and the options become fewer and fewer. In time, we will have no choices left. This is no idle threat; it is a pattern that repeats in history again and again.

Time says: "Now is the time to stir up knowledge!" We reply: "We cannot know, we should not see, we will not ask!" Knowledge comments: "Look carefully into the consequences! Ask where these limits come from. Do not believe others. Do not believe yourself! Do not believe at all—inquire!"

If we decide to inquire into the nature of time, what *kinds* of replies will we accept? Is our task to sort through all the answers given by human disciplines, to tally up the different theories, and select the candidate with the most votes? Or shall we ask ourselves what we personally think? In either case, we must ask why we would adopt that methodology. What distinctions are we making, and what is our basis for comparison? Whose authority are we accepting? Who verifies our knowledge? Who signed *his* diploma? Which state stamped and sealed it? Was it the state of confusion, the state of closed-mindedness, the state of fear?

If we are careful to exercise knowledge at each stage of our inquiry, we may find a new and different critical path for knowledge. We need not go in circles or down-ward spirals if the momentum of the inquiry is tuned in to the aliveness of time, time as immediately available experience. Perhaps we can ask time itself to grow knowledge of time, refining speculation to precision and imagination to vision.

Ordinary Time

Time is fascinating, but it moves too fast for us to take hold of it. Conventional understanding of past, present, and future seems unable to capture the momentum of time. Our fundamental questions are left unanswered.

One of the simplest questions we can ask is whether time is moving or we are moving through time. Is time like a river that carries our life raft along, or is it a corridor through which we move? How can we make a distinction between our moving and time moving? What does it mean to speak of movement in connection with time at all?

Right now galaxies are spinning, planets are orbiting. The universe is on the move, and we are along for the ride. Here on earth, we measure time passing according to the cycles of the earth moving around the sun: objective time in the physical world.

Strangely, these time measures are all relative to where we are in space. Our 2 PM in America is 2 AM in Asia. How difficult this might have been to explain to people long ago. Today, however, many of us have the experience of stepping off the plane at midnight 'my time' and noon 'their time'. It makes sense to us to say that at this moment, at different places on the earth, we are at different times.

If we shift perspective, this dependence of time on place can come to seem strange again. Imagine we are on Mars, looking down at earth. We ask: "What time is it now?" No matter whether the moon is in the Asian sky and the sun is in the American sky, isn't it really the same moment? Isn't that earth moment the same as this present moment here on Mars? Is there some fundamental time we are trying to point at when we measure out the hours? Isn't 'now' the same though one place is dark, the other is light, and the third geared to a different cycle entirely?

If we were to travel to another solar system, once we arrived, we would gear our measurement of time to the motions of the local stars and planets. But on the way back to earth, in outer space between the two star systems, how could we measure time at all? Whatever system we chose, it would seem rather arbitrary. Do these measurements have anything to do with time?

Imagine sitting perfectly still at a particularly quiet moment. All visible objects are unmoving; not a cloud passes in the sky, not a leaf blows in the wind. Yet even in this completely peaceful atmosphere, something is still moving. Is it time or is it us? Our heart is beating, our breath is flowing in and out, our thoughts and feelings are coming and going. Experience is moving, always, all the time.

If we are walking through the park, we easily sense the passing of time as connected to the passing of the scenery. If our body is still, we judge by our own thoughts moving: We know our thought just now is different from our thought a moment ago. In either case, we say with confidence: "Time has passed." Consider how this more intimate sense of time must somehow mesh with the time of the physical universe, as though two clocks were being synchronized. There must be different clocks for different living organisms related to their life spans or other timelines. Must not a fly take birth, grow to maturity, and die according to a time measured differently than ours? Measured time seems relative, manifold, and synchronized. Still, the mind conceives of a real and single 'now'.

INVESTIGATING THE PAST

How do we make distinctions between the past, present, and future? Where do we draw the line? Exactly how does the mind perceive the past, or does it only indirectly infer it?

When we think of the past, we are usually connecting to specific memories; because the memories are present, we assume something (the past events) must have created them. Can we look into the 'pastness' of time in a more direct way?

We might say that the presence of the memory is undeniable. Where would the memory come from if not from a past event? A memory presents itself as a trace of something that actually happened; that is what sets it apart from other images. If I imagine an apple and remember eating an apple at lunch, these two mental events are distinguishable, even though there may be quite some overlap between the generic apple and the memory of apple-eaten-at-lunch. Memory arrives with the distinctive 'feel' of a snapshot. Even though we know our memories of a few hours ago are partial and faulty, we still are convinced that they trace to a former present.

THE FEEL OF THE IMAGE

T his description raises two important questions: First, how is the 'feel' of a memory created around an image so that we can distinguish it from a similar image in our imagination? And second, where did that former present go?

The 'feel' of the past in memory might be described as present-that-isn't-anymore. It is one way we sense the pastness of time. The only 'place' that a memory snapshot can be taken is in the present, but that present is gone, that moment finished. The pastness of time is the 'goneness' of the present, the 'finishedness' of the moment. If we try recalling a series of memories from today or yesterday (for example, 10 AM, noon, 2 PM, and 4 PM), can we find the common 'feel' in all the images?

Can we also feel their differences, not in terms of image itself, but in terms of 'pastness'? How do we array them in the right order? How does the 10 AM image get oriented as 'paster' than the 4 PM image?

We could explore more fully by looking at memories of a present-that-isn't, but was just a moment ago. How close can we get? Here is a moment, and here in the next moment I check the snapshot of that past moment. This is very difficult to do if we are sitting quietly in a room with no activities, because there is not enough difference between the snapshot of the past and the present moment. The memory does not seem to show up clearly. If we try this same exercise walking, we may see more clearly how we tell the difference between the memory of the previous moment and the newly arising present moment. How and where do we draw the line? Can we find a difference between the present-that-isn't and the memory? What if our previous present moment was 'spent' looking at the memory of the moment that preceded it?

As we work with this exercise, we realize we are exploring two dimensions of time together—looking at the 'edge' between the present and the past. We are also looking into our other question: Where did that former present (the one we have the memory of) go, and how do we experience its 'goneness'? Experience suggests at least two possible answers: that the previous present disappears, or that it turns into a new moment. Both of these descriptions, and perhaps several others, could be investigated at length in our own direct experience.

What exactly is disappearing? Where does what 'go'? What turns into what?

DRAWING CLOSER TO TIME

A ctively inquiring into the structure of time in this way, either by focusing directly on the disappearing present, or on how memory images are different from other images, may allow us to draw closer to time itself. The act of investigating, the framing of a precise question, exercises knowledge. It begins almost immediately to strengthen the natural intelligence of the mind, to stimulate its curiosity and interest. As one question leads to the next, new avenues of inquiry open spontaneously. There is a growing sense of penetrating into the subject of inquiry. Time begins to disclose its workings to knowledge.

In our present inquiry, a difference begins to emerge between contacting memories of the past and contacting the 'pastness' of time itself. Our ordinary experience of the past seems to be a rather random recycling of memories. It happens all the time, bidden or unbidden. But carefully exploring the structure beneath, around, or within these images reveals time in a different, more direct way.

The dynamic of time exposed in this way—the dynamic momentum that moves moment into moment —is not sensory in the manner of a "square blue patch" reported by the senses. But we seem to be able to sense it within experience, provided we can activate knowledge that wishes to look into it carefully.

INVESTIGATING THE FUTURE

We could explore the future in a similar manner. If experiencing is rooted in the present, how do we know the future is not just our imagination? What exactly do we mean by future time? We often imagine the future, anticipating the events of the next hour or the evening's plans. We know we are thinking about something that has not happened yet. The future is what has not taken place—events that have not yet unfolded in space and may never occur just as we have imagined them.

At the same time, the future that becomes present is not random; there is some kind of precise sequencing. The future flower is connected to the present seed in a series of stages.

Can we separate out the 'futureness' of the future from our thoughts about it? What happens when we try to specify the exact differences between our thinking of a future event, for example, walking from one room into another, and the actual taking place of that event? Again, one is an image, while the other is the 'real scenery'. The real scenery is always in the present. Does this mean we do not experience the future? Does it mean that the 'futureness' of time is just our thoughts about the not-yet-happened?

When we imagine a future action, we get an image that is not unlike a memory. We know the difference between this future imagination and a memory because somehow the future imagination does not present itself as a record of an event that has already happened. It does not have the specific 'feel' of a memory.

How do we get a picture of something that did not take place yet? We just make it up! We can invent a 'filmstrip' of walking toward the kitchen, based on memories of hallway and kitchen. Yet even though the future imagination is based on past images, it does not feel like a memory; it feels like a possible future event.

How does an image come to have a forward projection rather than a backward projection in our imagination? How is it that we readily know the difference between these two directions, even when the images are almost identical, and even when we are fairly sure the future-oriented image is based on past models?

Suppose we recall eating breakfast yesterday and imagine eating the same breakfast tomorrow. We can tell the difference because our own connection to the event is gathered into the 'feel' of the image. Perhaps exploring that connection is a good way to deepen our inquiry.

EDGES OF TIME

T o look at the emergent future, the one that actually takes place as distinct from future imaginations, we could start with simple sensory experience of the present, focusing at the edge of 'now' just as it 'moves' into the future—the border where old gives way to new. In direct experience, new things are happening every moment. A sound, a motion, a sensation appears. Not everything is new, however: There is also a sense of continuity. Something stays the same and something changes, all in a very precise ratio.

Focusing on change and continuity in our moment to moment experience seems to bring us closer to the dynamic of time. Right here in the present, we must track the previous moment, the so-called past, holding it in memory long enough to tell that something has changed. At the same time, we must be letting go of the previous present so as to invite the incoming present, the so-called future. This holding and letting go, this tracking and inviting must happen very rapidly, almost simultaneously.

Perhaps it is like quickly passing a ball back and forth from one hand to the other. Is it possible to actually note the holding and the letting go? The transition between past-present and present-future is very rapid, the momentum unstoppable and unobstructed. It does not seem to depend on any conscious or deliberate act on our part.

Can we see clearly what is going on? If not, is the problem that there is not enough 'time between' moments? Or is it that the edges of moments are not distinct? Is time behaving this way because space is too tight? Knowledge too fuzzy? Is time's momentum being forced into line instead of having free reign?

CROSSROADS OF TIME

Ordinary perception simply seems unable to bring into experience the power and richness of time in its completeness. We depend on past memories and future-oriented projections, together with calculation and inference, but we do not *see* future or past. We experience three dimensions in space at once, but in time this seems impossible. Our thoughts of the future and memories of the past all seem to fall elsewhere 'along the same line' as the present in which we are experiencing.

Imagine Time teasing us: "How can you ever know what is in front of you? You come at the future from the backside of the future point. The front side of the past is the backside of the present, and the front side of the present is the backside of the future. You may know 'from' very well, but not 'to'. Your future is past tense too!"

As we experience them, 'pastness' and 'futureness' hover at the edges of the present. Exercising awareness seems to give a little access to these dimensions, like opening a door just a crack. Could we develop ways to imagine, sense, or inhabit time's dimensions of past, present, and future with more precision and finer resolution? If so, experience might deepen many times over, opening up new lines of inquiry that could lead into the heart of time.

Space-Time Partnership

S pace and Time are trying to establish priorities. Space says to Time: "I hired you! Before I came along to exhibit appearance, you had no job." Time replies: "Without my dynamic, you would be stuck where you are, completely stagnant!"

Now it is Time's turn. Time says to Space: "Without me, you are just zero, completely flat." Space replies: "Hah! Try manifesting your 'dynamic' without me! What can you do without any 'through'?"

If space needs time and time depends on space, then our inquiry into time will have to make some place for space, too. If space did not provide the place, how could the river of time flow or the corridor of time open? Yet, without time, the things of space could not change, grow, or evolve.

Space accommodates time, which likes to move, while time brings vitality to space. Together they bring forth everything in our world, including us. Our bodies are constructions of space and time, our minds re-flections of space and time.

SPACE WITHOUT TIME

When a point moves, a line defining one dimension appears. When the line moves, the two dimensions of a plane appear. When the plane moves, the three dimensions of a solid appear. 'Time to move' seems essential to the opening of dimensions.

Biology tells us that our perception of the depth dimension of ordinary space is the result of stereoscopic vision. Images from each eye, which are located in two slightly different positions, are synthesized by the brain into a single image compiled from different angles. It is as though we had moved slightly from one position to another, or as if we could occupy two positions at once! Depth depends on motion.

We might explore the dimensionality of space by looking very simply at what is in our visual field right now. Just as an artist might study the precise forms before his eye to translate them to a flat surface, we could note where one shape ends and the next begins. One color borders the next with no gap—there is no "space-colored space" in between the blue sky and the green tree. The space before us is completely filled with color and form. Sometimes we think of space as the absence of objects, the space in between the objects, or the place where nothing 'is', the not-something in between all the many 'somethings'. But if we observe from one position without moving, such an 'absence' or 'in-between' will never manifest.

If we simply stand still and look, depth seems to collapse. We have right and left, up and down, but no 'to' and 'from'. Looking out on the landscape what we actually see is smaller and larger shapes. Distance seems to be an interpretation imposed upon this experience. Likewise, we see shadow and light, but contour seems to be interpretation.

But as soon as I start to move, something changes. I seem to be walking *through* space, through a transparent medium. The 'through' of space and the motion of time are intimately connected. Moving, I see the tree before me from different angles, and its depth becomes apparent. Another dimension opens up. The question arises: What if we could move differently, in another kind of space? Would other dimensions of time open up? Suppose we think of time as a kind of space. Is it possible to rotate a point of time? Turn a line of time? Shift a plane of time?

TIME WITHOUT SPACE

Could the present moment happen non-spatially? Could experience take place without any place? Imagine some state of consciousness where there is no form of space apparent, perhaps some formless meditative realm. No outer space would be perceived, and thus no colors, forms, lights, shadows, or dimensions. No inner space would be perceived either: no space for the breath to flow, the heart to beat, or the head to ache.

What about the space where our thoughts flow? Though we may not know the precise nature of that mental arena, it seems to share qualities with physical space, being the 'place' where thoughts are allowed extension and memories and images appear. Let's imagine that this mental space for various activities also closes down.

At this point, it seems that all perception and experience would simply stop, not unlike deep sleep. The meditator emerging from such an experience may look at his watch and note that time has passed, but within that state with nothing changing in space, how could he know time's passing?

What could experience be like if it were allowed no space in which to happen? No matter how strong the momentum of time or the desire to move and flow, where could any dance begin? Perhaps we can imagine one moment appearing as a point without dimensions. But how could that moment connect to the next if there is no 'through' of space in which time could flow? Would the energy of time just keep pumping into that single point for billions of years? But how could we even count the years if there were no space in which something moved or vibrated to be tracked and measured? If time's flow depends on space's 'through', how could perception take place? Without space, could light travel from object to eye? Could impulses flow from eye to brain? Could anything be known at all?

We have been assuming that one moment of time is connected to the next, though we do not know the mechanism. Now we see that time must connect to space at the same time! Moments flow and movement takes place in space. It seems that space and time must be united for time to perform.

CLOSENESS OF TIME AND SPACE

The marriage of space and time is clearly reflected in ordinary knowledge. We count out time by measuring space. One day is a specific number of miles of earth-travel around the sun. We also count out time to measure space. "The store is a five-minute walk from here." And "How long?" is a question that may be directed toward either space or time.

To specify that something exists, we need to know both where it is and when it is, its coordinates in space and time. Could something exist in space without having a place in some kind of time? Could something physical exist in time but not have a place in some kind of space?

No matter how accommodating and inviting space might be, if there were no time, the universe would not expand or contract, the world would not spin. When we speak of time as a fourth dimension, it may seem that space is three times more important than time. But time's dynamic is no afterthought, no extra in the play of space.

CLOSER THAN CLOSE

If space and time are not two, why do we think of them as separate? Perhaps it is because we are used to thinking in terms of 'thingness'. Ordinary knowledge sees time as a river, a flowing stream of moments that pass by one after the other, and it sees space as the sky, a blank canvas, a vacuum. Tied to these images, we cannot comprehend the unity of space and time. How can a river be intimately linked to a canvas? The question of when and the question of where, we say, are different questions.

But if we look into the 'here/there' dichotomy of space that makes up the 'where' and the 'now/then' division of time that makes up the 'when', we cannot separate them. United, they create the 'from/to'. . . 'from/to'. . . 'from/to'. . . succession of space-time. Every 'from' is a point in space *and* time, and so is every 'to'. 'Here' implies 'now' and 'there' implies 'then'. The structure that supports this is the 'I am here'. Both 'here' and 'now' belong to the speaker. They travel with the 'I' wherever it goes.

Space declares: "I am here." Time adds: "I am now." *I am here now.* Can we have 'here' without 'now'? Can we have 'now' without 'here'? Both are signs of life.

Space and time seem closer than fire and heat. How can this be? We might better ask: How can this not be? Do we think that space allows any distance between space and time? Do we imagine that time must move closer to embrace space?

Coming to Be

Although space gives directions, all directions lead back to the natural openness of zero. For time, the meaning is that everything is possible. There are no zoning laws in operation, no barriers or checkpoints, no previous occupancy and no off-limits. Time activates the 'can' that space allows, and through such 'timeability', existence comes to be.

Time brings alive what space can do. Unfolding the cone, it makes appearance available for knowledge to explore. Its rhythms of repetition and newness reflect the repeating structures of space. As transition depends on form and form on transition, time and space rely on one another to give birth to what is.

The child Existence inherits equally from Mother Space and Father Time. We could think of points and lines and cones and 16 as the genes that pass on this inheritance. But just because one possibility takes form and matures does not mean that others are excluded. Many things are happening in all directions.

Speaking in a simple way, we might say that the 16 of space and the 16 of time join to produce the 16 of what there is; of what is there. Physical existence and phenomena are there! How do they develop? Through time and space. When did they develop? Through time and space. In our kind of time and space, there are objects, and objects are there, but in the end it is all time and space.

If we say that space has a body, that body is full openness, without ownership or exclusion. Through the power of time, the body of space comes to be; through time and space together, being develops.

The power of timing is beyond our calculations! Yet we know that it matches quite precisely the openness of space. The dynamic of time synchronizes with the territory of space, with nothing left over: a time-space harmony of equilibrium. In such a bonding, there will be no ratio, no outside force that shapes or separates or measures. There can be no disruption or adjustment. Time and space together give the ratios for all and everything, but between them there is no 'between'.

Time and space need no interpreters or mediators. They are instantly together; they make their mark. From that marriage, knowledge makes its point and tells its story. But the story remains symbolic, for all that contributes to form has never departed from the zero-point of space.

Relying on the 'there', the 'I am here' enters the story as actor and as narrator, and tells us what is so. In one sense, it is sheer fabrication. In another sense, the 'here' that the story sets in place opens into depths beyond what we imagine. Here is the observer; here is awareness; here is the knowing of being. Here is full time-space comprehension.

Endpoints
of Time

Once we have located a point in space, we know it must also have a time. We might say the starting point of space and time are somehow the same point. Time and space must expand and grow together.

To establish a point in space, the first step is to find the baseline in time as well. We need to know where we are measuring from. From 'now', of course. We are in time 'now', looking toward some other point, 'then.' Just as the line between 'here' and 'there' is the baseline in space, the line between 'now' and 'then' is the baseline of time.

In space we located a zero-point using the axes, two lines marking four directions that specified the point like an x. Would the time-point share the same four axes? Would it have its own axes? Would they overlap or coalesce with the axes of the point in space?

The baseline is a timeline that extends from 'now' to 'then'. To locate a point on that line, we have to cross the line with another, just as we did with space. In this way, we can mark off notches or grooves to designate the passing of time: in seconds, minutes, hours, years, or centuries. We can measure 'before' and 'after', 'then' and 'now', and any other ordinary point in time. Looking at a Thursday, we know that 2 PM is before 3 PM and after 1 PM. We can narrow these limits down to seconds, or even finer divisions. Before 2:00:01 and after 1:59:59 locates more precisely the time point being indicated.

How do we determine the endpoints of this baseline of time? In asking this question, we should remember that we are not in the position of an observer outside the timeline. We are one of the endpoints, 'now'. This gives us half our answer. The other endpoint must be at the beginning of time, a point it makes sense to designate as zero. But can we actually say where this zero is located? Clearly, we must move the point back to the 'beginning' of the line, but where is that? Wherever we put the point, we should put it before that. What we want is the endpoint of the line, the zero from which the line emerged. Is such a point available?

Whenever someone in history has inquired into the beginning of time, they have been looking for that same zero-point. Where we are today was their future, but according to the standard account, their pasts and ours have the same beginning point. They are 'behind' us on the timeline, and we are 'ahead' of them. Interestingly, the zero-point of this line seems fixed, but we have to constantly update the endpoint 'now'. The line is always growing longer. How sure are we about all this? What evidence can we point to?

BEGINNING AND ENDING OF TIME

O ur timeline emerges from zero and proceeds on— for billions of years—up to now. Do we imagine it will stop at some point 'later'? Is it the nature of time to start but not stop? It does not seem quite acceptable to say that something begins but does not come to an end; at least we have no model for such a structure, nor does it match our ideas of cause and effect.

We might speculate that time is everlasting, but somehow shimmers or shifts, creating what we call past, present, future. Or we might imagine that the nature of time is eternal, but that its power comes forth as temporariness and temporality. This would lead us into an exploration of the relationship between the nature of time and its manifestation, their connection, the means of manifesting, the timing of that manifestation, and so forth. In the end, it seems we would arrive back at the question of beginnings after all.

NEGATIVE TIMELINE

P erhaps there is another way to look at beginnings and endings. In being the beginning of time, the zero-point may not be an endpoint of time in the way we have been imagining. The starting point of time that we have thus far envisioned is the beginning of a long timeline that starts at 'one side' of zero and goes up to 'now'. Recalling the axes that locate the zero-point in space, however, we realize that we have forgotten the other side of the line, the 'other side' of the zero-point.

To speak of the sides of the zero-point is to consider the direction of time. Our experience of time is that it flows in one direction, from 'then' to 'now'. The zero-point of time must have at least one side, one gateway, one door going out. But if it has a front, might it not have a back?

What kind of timeline might emerge from the back side of the zero-point of time? On mathematical axes, the left side of zero is reserved for negative values. Can we conceive of a negative timeline emerging from the other side of the starting point? The idea has a kind of visual logic to it, but does it have any substance? How would negative time be measured? In degrees of impossibility, or incompleteness, or non-realization? Could this line somehow be the reverse of the positive side of time, a time that flowed backward? We have no reason to accept any of these possibilities. Perhaps we can simply leave the back of zero truly open, remembering that there may be a side of time we do not now know.

RIVER OF TIME

Our experience of time presents us with directionality, distinctions, and irreversibility. The present is now, ongoing, while the future is yet to come and the past has already happened. The past used to be the present, and the present will become the future. The past feels like it is behind us, the future seems to be ahead, and we are in the middle, here in the present. In this image, the past is the source from which the present arises, and the present is the source from which the future will arise. Causes in the past give rise to effects in the future. Like a mountain stream, the past flows downhill, its current the present, heading toward the unknown ocean of the future.

However, we sometimes think of time flowing in the other direction. The future is coming toward us and the past is receding away from us while we are positioned here in the present. In this image, we are pointed upstream at the future, with the wake of the past receding behind us.

How is it possible to imagine time in two completely opposite ways? In one case we seem to be moving along with the flow of time going from past to future. In the other case, we seem to be a rock situated in the stream with the future rushing toward us. Can we switch back and forth from one view to the other? Is the 'feel' of 'pastness' and 'futureness' different? And what of the present?

OTHER SIDE OF ZERO

In our imaginations, can we reverse the flow of time that has led from the beginning to the present? Can we run the film backwards? Would we see the galaxies condense into primeval energies that converge on a single point, like water swirling down a drain? As we go back billions and billions of years, space would shrink and time would flow backwards. Without concerning ourselves too much with the details of the cosmology, it seems we would reach a place where space has no dimension and time is not moving.

But why should time stop? Does it run into something? Does it lose power? Does space get so small that time has no room to move? Or does time not stop at all? Does it go through the doorway of zero and continue out the other side?

CONE OF HISTORY

T o model the long history of our universe, we could imagine a cone of space-time projecting out of a zero-point, expanding in space as it moves through time. In the present, we occupy a point on the face of the cone, while the past points back toward the starting point. The length of the cone is the measure of time elapsed 'since the beginning', while the diameter of the face is the measure of space expansion. The sides of the cone extend and the circular face expands, manifesting the momentum of time and the accommodation of space. From subatomic particles to planets, from atoms to galaxies, all our known history is within this cone: all cells, plants, and animals, all civilizations, governments, philosophies, and religions, all music, art, medicine, and law. All of our history, our dreams, imaginations, and thoughts—all of our known universe is within this cone.

But if we can imagine a cone emerging from one side of a zero-point, what of the other sides? If a cone radiates from the front side, why not the back? Does it seem a bit shocking to imagine the other side of zero with real dimensions and a real unfolding dynamic, rather than as a blank or abstraction? Or does it make some kind of sense?

Back to
the Beginning

I magine traveling back in space and time to the beginning of the universe. Logic suggests that in our present day, the oldest materials of the universe are at the fringes, having had the longest time to travel, while the materials at the center are younger. Does this mean we should set out for the center of the universe, looking for some specific point in space that is the scene of the original Big Bang, like the base of an enormous branching tree spreading in all directions?

Something in the picture seems wrong. If our universe is expanding from the beginning point of space-time, it is expanding in all directions at once. There would not be any stable ground in which the tree could take root. Could there even be a root, or would there just be branches in all directions?

On the other hand, a search for a beginning point 'makes sense'. Is this sense based on logic or on experience? In everyday experience, things stop and start all the time. They arise, continue for a while, and then come to an end. It seems that time itself tells us stories with beginnings and endings. But could time tell such a tale about itself? Is time a thing in time? Is time 'outside' of time? When the story teller tells his last story, does he fall silent? Does he disappear?

TIME 'PRIOR TO'

W hen it comes to time, the whole idea of a starting point is troublesome. For something to start, there must be a time before it starts, a 'prior'. Suppose there is such an ancestor to time: What would be prior to the beginning? How could you point out 'prior' if there is not yet any timeline of 'before/after' and 'now/then'? If time is a necessary condition for existence, then what could possibly exist to serve as the ancestor? How could time's ancestor and time as its descendent be connected? Whether we say the birth of time took place all at once or in stages, it still seems to take time.

If ordinary knowledge is based on distinctions that all derive from prior experience, how can it apply in a realm prior to 'prior'? Could it even frame the right kinds of questions to point to new understanding? Our past-based knowledge says we want to know about the origin of time—as though we wanted time to present us with the proper records from long ago, to dig up its birth certificate from the trunks in the basement. Why does it seem so unlikely this will work? Is it simply that time will not sit still for it? Or are there other conditions operating that we might explore?

NOT KNOWING 'TO' AND 'FROM'

When we hit such barriers to understanding, does it mean our language is limited, our thought limited, our imagination limited? Does it mean that time is somehow contradictory? Unknowable?

Perhaps we need to stop and ask where our logic of 'to' and 'from', 'before' and 'after' comes from and what it is based on. When we look into time, are we really looking into the architecture of the human mind?

Suppose we answer the question in the negative. What would it mean to make a distinction between time itself and the structure of the mind that is attempting to know time? Our ideas of 'to' and 'from' must come *from* somewhere, but we may not know from where. Are our ideas based on knowing or on not-knowing? If they are based on knowing, what exactly do we know, and how do we know it? If they are based on not-knowing, exactly what do we not know? Maybe we do not know how to investigate thoroughly, or what to ask. Maybe we are ignorant of where to look or how to sense different layers of experience.

Can we tell how many of our human constructions we might be projecting onto time? If we do not know the ratio of mental constructs to time itself, how can we investigate the question?

What conclusion can we draw from all these impenetrable questions? Having started down the road of inquiry, shall we throw up our hands? Is it time to make an about-face and retire from the arena of knowledge, muttering: "That's the way it is! That's the human condition! The world is a mystery!"

Where do *these* conclusions come from? What theory of human nature are we adhering to? We seem about to enter a world view that comes complete with its own time, space, and knowledge, its own architecture, its own history, and its own axioms. Seeing this, we might step back out the door into the open, continuing to inquire into our not-knowing.

As children say: "How come? How come?" How does it come about that the nature of time appears unknowable and mysterious to us? Can we detect the conditions that guide us to this conclusion? If we recognize that we do not know, perhaps new knowledge can grow *from* the seed of not-knowing. Perhaps not-knowing opens another angle on 'to' and 'from'.

TIME TO BE

One thing we seem to know is that time is necessary for existence. For anything to exist, it must have time to appear and space to emerge. For existence to exist, space and time are prerequisites. It takes time to take place. We might say that the background of existence is space and time.

Whether it is random or not random, part of a causal sequence or not, experience takes place in time, not outside of time. Time to be produced, time to manifest, time to be perceived, time to be recognized, time to be known, time to become part of our physical universe, our histories and our stories. Likewise, when time runs out, existence comes to an end. When the time for something is gone, it cannot be recalled. Not one more day can be squeezed out, not one more moment is left. No time, no existence!

Let us consider our own timeline, our own existence and non-existence. Here time is no philosophical conundrum, but literally a life-and-death question. How did our time begin? Where were we before we were? How is it possible that our time will stop? Time warns us: "'Now' is time to be; 'then' will be time not to be." The deadline cuts through the timeline like a knife.

Beginnings and endings are not abstractions but facts of life. Can we remember this? Can we use this realization to throw ourselves into the inquiry at a different angle?

THE 'FROM' OF TIME

If time sets the conditions for our lives, we have the right to know where it gets its authority. Where did time get its power over us? Where did time get its power at all? Who is the producer of time? Who gave birth to it? Who initiated it and sponsored it? Who gave it permission to begin? Facing up to time, we say: "I am here now! Who are you, back then, to run my life?"

Perhaps we have forgotten where we are measuring from. Looking for the starting point, we have been pounding on a door that is billions of years away from 'here' and 'now'. But if I do not know time 'here', how can I find out 'there'? Is there even any way to know whether there is any 'there' there without a 'here' here?

I am here. We cannot ignore the observer. Atoms may tick without us, molecules may meet and part without our observation, but when we try to cut off the observer completely, we create an abstraction. We have imagined in our inquiry into the beginning that we have leaped off the timeline, but the two points, the two ends, are inseparable.

In fact, they are in certain ways interchangeable. From the point of view of the fruit, the seed is its starting point. From the point of view of the seed, the fruit is its starting point. Is the Big Bang the starting point or are we the starting point? It all depends. At different eras in history, the empire of England or China may claim to be the center of the universe, but an observer on Mars would not for a moment weigh the merits of the two cases.

HERE'S STORY OF THERE

We have seen that 'here' implies 'there', 'now' implies 'then'. Why are these pairs so bound together? We try to separate them with a long line of time or space, but they refuse to part ways.

The story of 'then' requires some study, for it is actually quite strange. We say, "Now I will sleep, and then I will work." Here, 'then' specifies the future element in a sequence, the 'this' that comes after 'that'. But we can also say: "Then I did not understand, but now it is clear to me." Now we have made 'then' refer to a prior moment in time.

'Then' is always some other time than 'now'. It is the 'not-now' that actually defines 'now', the negative film that creates the positive print. 'Now' and 'not-now' define each other—or we might say that the line between them defines them both. How does this line get drawn?

Ordinary knowledge needs a starting point in time, just as it does in space. It seeks the first of the series. Having located that point, 'back then', or 'over there', we move through time and space in our imagination to explain how 'here' comes about from 'there', how 'now' comes from 'then'. The story we tell describes how time unfolds. It puts events in sequence to make a coherent account, not only in terms of before and after, but usually in terms of cause and effect as well.

From my position here and now, I imagine starting from there, back then. If the story is well told (for instance, backed up with logic or convictions), it may not present itself as a story at all, but as "This is the way it was." The 'was' is meant to found our present 'is', but it is also based on the present 'is'. 'Here' is where the measurements are taken, the ideas developed, the data put together, the hypotheses tested and refined.

Every era tells its story to arrive at the 'was' of its 'is', using the best tools at its command. But although the histories all turn out differently, the basic element remains the same: a starting point 'then' and a line of time that leads from 'there' to 'here', from 'then'—whenever that may be—to 'now'.

If this seems abstract, we might try bringing the story closer to home. *I am here now*, wondering where I come from. I assume I have a 'before', a 'then', a history. How could I be here without a past? Looking directly into this story in its being told, we can touch the timed-out nature of the self and its identity through time—the founding story of all stories told by the self, the hidden temporal structure of the 'am'.

Unraveling the deeper layers of 'now' and 'then', 'from' and 'to' stimulates questions. We do not have to let these questions immediately generate a history or a mystery. Instead, their asking can energize and focus awareness.

Knowledge and time begin a dialogue right in our midst. How does 'now' imply all times? How can it be that being is 'now'? Starting right now, I can look into existence and time together. My 'am' is that space where knowledge and time intersect.

Dimensions
of Time

What if instead of a single starting point, there were many starting points in space and time? Suppose that any here and now could be a zero-point. What would this tell us about time?

The symbol of 16 speaks of the wholeness that resides in the zero-point. And indeed, if a starting point is not in some sense a whole, how can it be a seed? Let us imagine the zero-point, where the two lines of the axes cross, as a whole. Space has presented the image: The axes rotate, four directions become eight, then sixteen: a sphere with 16 lines in all directions, an image of the whole of time as well as space.

It is not hard to imagine 16 lines radiating from a point of space, for we can readily visualize a sphere. But a spherical point in time, a point with many sides, may seem much harder to make sense of. How many sides does time truly have? All we know now are past, present, and future, and it is hard to represent even these three dimensions in three-dimensional form.

The three dimensions of space are spatially present simultaneously, but time seems to hide the future and the past from view, revealing only the present. We locate time-points on one line only, along which we string all of past, present, and future. The three divisions of time run together; their edges do not seem distinct. Time's directionality seems to give a one-dimensional structure.

Could we imagine locating a point along three time-lines simultaneously, in the way a spatial point can be located in three dimensions? Ordinary knowledge replies confidently that a point in time can only be situated in one dimension, for that is the way human experience unfolds. To be past is defined precisely as the not-present and the not-future; to be future is precisely not-past and not-present.

The ring of finality is suspicious. Perhaps our sense of time's threefold dimensionality has been flattened. Why should time be compressed into a single dimension that belongs nowhere? Why are we compelled to travel in a tube heading one direction, instead of being allowed to roam freely in time? Is it enough to say that this is the way things are?

Where would we look for more sides to time, for different directions or dimensions? One approach might be to be more precise about the dimensions we already know. Each moment of time must have a beginning, middle, and end. Just as the present has a past, present, and future, perhaps the past has a past, present, and future, and the future also. If these dimensions were to meet with one another, we might suspect that time would "break to pieces." But they might coordinate with one another and with space.

Where would these connections take place? In a fourth dimension? There is a symmetry in this suggestion. Apply the fourth dimension of time to each of the three dimensions of time, and there are four dimensions, each with four dimensions. So we arrive at 16 after all.

Whether these speculations can sustain themselves or not is not the point. We are asking after a symbol of wholeness: discrete and precise directions radiating from the zero-point of time. If lines do not flow out in some such way, how can the zero-point possess the complete power of time?

TRIANGLE OF TIME

T he image of 16 lines radiating from the zero-point of time encourages an investigation into the shape of a moment. Can we imagine the sides and angles of a moment of time? Could points of time have an up, down, and sideways, as well as a forward and backward?

If we think of time being divided into past, present, and future, we can easily imagine time as a triangle, with the points of past and future marking the base and the present point above. From that present point 'above', we look forward toward the future and back toward the past. In each moment, a new triangle forms, a new present point in between past and future.

Following the suggestion made above about dimensions within dimensions, we could imagine that at each angle of the triangle there is a smaller triangle representing the past, present, and future of the past, the past, present, future of the present, and the past, present, future of the future.

POINT TO POINT

Time as a stream or flow of moments suggests a model in which perception skims the surface of time, moving from point A to point B to point C, each in the present. Can we say if there is anything between the points? Can we account for how one point connects to the next, making the flow of experience possible?

What would be the right spatial analogy for the flow of time? Are moments strung along a thread? If so, what constitutes the thread? Is there a linking rod that does not run through the moments themselves? Are moments joined directly side to side or front to back like balls glued together? Are they linked by some kind of gravity or force field? Could the fields of each moment overlap? Could one moment grow from another moment, the way cells divide? Does one moment give birth to another as though from out of itself, the way children are born? Our ordinary experience does not reveal any 'between'—just one present somehow 'merging' into the next.

The suggestion that moments of time can be seen as triangles of past-present-future time complicates the picture still further. On the one hand, this seems like a meaningful analogy for our everyday experience. We operate only in the present, but beneath the present, behind or ahead of it, are the past and the future. But how do past and future link up?

Do A's future and B's past connect so that time can flow? Does one become the other? What if these are really two names for the same point?

BETWEEN POINTS

Seeing how hard it is to pin down the present moment and understand its functioning, it seems entirely possible that what we call a point or moment of time may not be the simplest, irreducible unit of time. In between the point A and point B that we recognize, there may be more points. The 'future' of A and the 'past' of B, for example, might be such points, 'existing' or available in different ways. But it is also possible that there are more 'present' moments between *any* two moments we specify. Our experience suggests this view, since we know that we do miss moments, for instance, when we are not concentrating well.

Suppose that perception could be trained to trace smaller and smaller divisions of time, so that we could capture more of its finer motions.* This might be like diving down between points on the surface. Would this mean discovering new triangles 'between' the old ones? Or would it mean exploring the triangle of each arising moment? In such an exploration, could we engage a different, more interesting rhythm than the strictly point-to-point linear motion that ordinary knowledge assigns to time?

TRIANGLES TO DIAMONDS

Once we allow that there might be more subtle dynamics within linear time, why confine ourselves to movement up and down? Could time take off at various angles to the ordinary timeline? Could it unfold at several angles simultaneously, the way a cone projects out of a point or a flower opens from a bud? For instance, what we conceive of or sense as the triangle of time might be just a face on a more fully dimensioned shape, such as a diamond. Perhaps we inhabit a vast and sparkling diamond network of moments, discrete and yet connected. Seen as one angle of such a network— one possibility for time's dynamic—the whole linear momentum of ordinary time would take on a different significance.

---

* For an exercise that develops this suggestion, see "Opening Time," *Dimensions of Thought I.* Berkeley: Dharma Publishing, 1980.

Depth of Time

S omething that exists takes time and takes up space. What does this 'take' mean? The object appears, filling up a certain amount of space and a specific duration in time.

Clearly, more than one thing can occur simultaneously within a specific point in time—many things have happened all over the world in the time of reading this sentence. 'Taking' time does not seem to imply exclusivity.

Surprisingly, more than one thing can also occur simultaneously at the same point in space. Events do not fill up space completely, for smaller events occur layered inside larger events. Layering is not like a building filled with rooms, with different activities underway in each room. Instead, think again of the human body. Inside the chest is the heart, inside the heart are cells, inside the cells are mitochondria and nuclei, inside the nuclei are DNA molecules, inside the molecules are atoms of carbon and hydrogen and nitrogen, and so forth. When we shift from macroscopic to microscopic, we are going *deeper* into space. What is happening in one layer of space is different from what is happening in another.

Is layering possible in time as well? Inside one hour are sixty minutes, but each one seems to have its separate place, like rooms along a corridor, arranged one after the other. We can break the minute up into seconds, but this would be analogous to partitioning the rooms. The structure remains linear, not layered.

Suppose, however, that we could step inside a cell. According to biologists, we would find that its clock seems to run on a different rhythm than ours. Cells can synthesize in a few minutes complex compounds that take many days to manufacture in the laboratory. How can the cell 'fit' all of that time into just a few of the minutes we know?

In the same way, we could speculate that atomic time must be very different from the light years of galactic time. The Theory of Relativity, which suggests that time can speed up or slow down, offers further support for the view that time operates differently at different 'levels'.

To explore this possibility, we would need a way of entering different layers of time, of changing the focal setting. One way might be through developing greater concentration, so that awareness penetrates the moment more precisely. Recalling the triangles of time, we might try diving into time, finding ways to explore the sequencing and flow differently. Can we take on this challenge? Can we find an hour in a single minute?

Unfolding the Cone

Let us return to the image of the cone that emerges from zero, taking it to represent our ordinary sense of time and space, with its boundedness and established directionality. Based on the possibilities we have been exploring, can we discover any ways to open this structure to inquiry?

In the cone of time starting with the Big Bang, the two directions of time seem very clear, backward and forward, 'from' and 'to', along the baseline from the starting point to now. The two ends are easily distinguishable as well, one infinitesimally small and the other incredibly large. Time seems to flow down the length of the baseline to open up enormous reaches of space here and now.

From another perspective, both ends are equally zero. The shape of the cone is maintained by these two zeros interacting, holding the lines of the cone between them. If we knew how to open up the zero at the apex and the zero at the face of the cone, would the sides of the cone unwind? Suppose we switched positions, making here and now the zero of the starting point. Would we still see the cone expanding from 'here' to 'there'? Where would the 'there' be and how far away? Or would the switch mean that the cone begins to unfold?

Another way to imagine unfolding the cone is by opening the angle on zero. Think of the way an umbrella opens: first thirty degrees, then ninety degrees, and then finally 180 degrees. We could imagine the sides of the cone expanding, umbrella-fashion, by unfolding more folds of 'fabric' tucked into the walls. What might the extra folds of time and space fabric be? Could there be more time and more space in the cone than we thought?

Perhaps the angle on the zero at the apex could keep opening past 180 degrees. Eventually, the cone would rotate completely around to the other side of zero, like an umbrella turned inside out. If the cone opened a full 360 degrees, its shape would disappear completely, leaving everything wide open, without bounds.

These images are only suggestive. The cone shape comes forth on the basis of zero, on the basis of the baseline and its endpoints, on the basis of the axes with their negative and positive sides, and the four directions times four. Each one of these originating factors might similarly become a key for opening our perspective beyond the cone. What might we rotate or unfold, expand or condense? There seems to be more than one way to open a cone.

RADIATING CONES

If each zero encompasses 16 lines of directionality, 16 zeros emerge, and cones could emerge in turn from all of the zeros simultaneously. This image of cones in

16 different directions makes us ask again if space and time have developed in only one direction. To us, the countless shapes and forms that have developed over billions of years seem a more than adequate display of time's power. But do we really think that everything that exists exists within our cone? Do we believe that time is on our side, but not on the other sides? Can we be certain that time is going in one direction only? Would two cones side by side share a 'wall' of time? Would two cones at opposite ends of an axis have any special relationship? If the cones emerging in 16 directions unfurled just the smallest amount, would they not begin to overlap or intersect one another?

RINGS IN TIME

I magine a zero-point giving rise to 16 cones, each cone able to branch out into another 16 cones. Eventually, this rhythm would fill the shape of a giant cone. Imagine 16 major sequences in this cone, detectable as rings along its surface. Some cones might be very long—perhaps billions of years. Looking inside a cone of great length, we might distinguish numerous patterns of smaller cones, reflecting steps in its development.

If we could examine the detailed records of such an unfolding from numerous perspectives, we might see, like images in time-lapse photography, a series of smaller cones getting larger and longer as our cone grew. Here is the infant cone, here the young cone, the adult, and so forth. Suppose the 16 rings are a pattern that repeats for all cones of all lengths of time. Each of the "younger" cones would have 16 stages, but all sizes of cones would be filled with smaller cones arrayed in all directions.

On a given cone, everything between two rings would share the same era of time, however long that might be. Different eras might be very different from one another, as transitions were made from ring to ring. Would the operations of time necessarily be the same in different rings of the cone? How would the stages be connected together in time, so that time could flow?

Can we imagine different cone-like structures for the time we call our universe's history, our planet's history, our continent's history, our country's history, our family's history, our personal history? Can we see how they fit within one another? Can we take the pattern to a smaller measure, seeing cones everywhere in time: in a day, an hour, a moment? Can we imagine unfolding these cones in different ways?

Each cone imagined in this way points to past sequences. Here and now, do we imagine all the patterns of the past are gone? Does all of time's past effort simply disappear into the present, vanishing without a trace, a sacrifice as past gives way to present?

Power of Time

If any point might be a starting point, each point could operate extraordinary complexity. How could all of that power, momentum, and sequencing be packed into any and every moment of time?

Within the cone as it takes shape, our experience is of gradual transitions. As time moves, its power is continuous, its momentum uninterrupted. The seed does not leap forward abruptly to become the fruit, but shifts from seed to plant to flower before the fruit can ripen. One form grows into another smoothly in small steps that flow into one another at varying rates.

Though seeming to expand in all directions through increasingly complex interconnections, the operations of time remain coordinated and connected. Change and continuity develop together. Time charges form to transform, and the old form seems to disappear as the new one takes shape. The two are the same and yet different, different and yet the same—the space wizardry of time.

How does the power of time actually operate these changes? We can imagine many stages in time, from points to small cones, to larger cones of all kinds, each marked with rings of development. Within any single cone there might also be a layering of different times within times. Somehow the momentum of time must be transmitted through all these transitions.

Each transition-point must also be a zero-point. Is this point of transition a 'new' starting point for the development of a new pattern, based on what came before? Would it have available an array of new choices, based on the development of time's linear dynamic up to that point? Or is it more likely that everything 'starts from zero' at each moment? Does time flash off and on, negative and positive, wholly present and creating the whole in each point?

Are the connections between layers and rings re-ducible to connections between tiny moments layered within the larger patterns? Can we conceive of how all these moments would coordinate with one another?

Imagine the cone developing in terms of the ratio of the length to the opening circular face. If we are think-ing along the lines of linear time, we might speculate that the 16 zero-points of the 16 cones are 'within' the zero-point, but do not manifest 'until' the cone reaches a certain level of development. How long does that take? Is this 'length' of time related to the length of the cone in linear time? How 'far away' are the two zeros of the cone? How can we measure? What is the line made of and how long does it take to traverse?

What if we do not think in terms of linear time, the time of the baseline and experience? Suppose it takes *no time* to move in any direction within the cone. After all, the cone unfolds 'from' zero 'to' zero, and there is nothing between the zeros but more zeros. Imagine 16 cones distributed 'around' a zero, the face of each cone another zero with another 16 points, each of which can manifest another cone. Can we envision simultaneous developments going on in all directions?

Between simultaneous and linear a contradiction operates. Perhaps this is a clue that our point of view does not yet have a wide enough angle. What if all times were connected together? What if time could move in all directions? Where might we discover the inner dynamics, the interconnections, and the transmission points in time? Suppose there is another time inside the time we know, a fourth dimension of time. If we could enter that time, would the mechanisms of time's magical abilities be differently illuminated?

MECHANISM OF PRECISION

Imagine that each point in time requires 16 transition points to reach completion. If the stages are not clear and distinct, precise connections could likely not be made. Without specificity, the event or object would not take form or else would not take form completely. Its development or manifestation would be stalled.

If time's dimensions did not reach the 16th degree, time's power would likewise remain diffuse, its momentum not focused and directed. Time would be unable to inspire, but could only push or drag. Depending on all the interconnections, it might move slowly or rapidly, smoothly or erratically, but it would not bring forth a clear form.

In contrast, once the full complement of the 16th degree has been reached, a transition can be made. If we see in terms of sequences, we might suppose another set of 16 begins to develop, a new series of possibilities not possible before the transition. If we do not see in terms of sequences, we might imagine 16s everywhere, all the time.

DYNAMIC OF BOUNDLESSNESS

Let us call 'zero' being, or let us call it space, time, and knowledge. Zero is the starting point: any point of space, time, and knowledge. If zero expands to 16, every 16 is zero and every zero is 16. Accordingly, 16 implies specificity, but also boundlessness, the perfectly fulfilled four times four, wide open in every direction. As an image for this open fulfillment, imagine a sphere with a mirrored surface cut into millions of facets, reflecting light in all directions simultaneously.

Zero as zero has no properties. But if zero has no property, how can it have an edge? An edge demarcates where one property stops and another starts. If zero has no edge or side, what lines could mark out its position?

How can it be established? How can it even be 'not established'?

If there were no transition from zero, nothing could appear or be known. But 16 allows for transition. 16 is a gateway through which space and time appear. But the transition of 16 may or may not appear. Zero may remain zero, or may manifest as particles and qualities.

In the development of space and time, all kinds of things can appear—as many as space allows and time develops in all directions limitlessly. Does all of this space-time development reside 'in' the zero-point? Do the layers of time truly allow for the compression of 'everything' into 'nothing'?

In the journey through matter to space, we can go to atoms, then to subatomic particles. Going further, we come to zero-space, and the honeycomb of matter becomes translucent. If we analyze time, something similar happens. We go to moments, then to submoments, then to zero-time. But in both cases, we do not arrive at zero without 16. Zero transitions to 16, allowing the transition to form.

OPERATION OF THE RATIO

We know from observation that the way our world changes is by reaching and then crossing thresholds that mark transitions. This transition can be expressed as a ratio, the precise relationship between various elements that allows the transition to take place.

The ratio specifies the degree of change. Millions of ratios specify discrete changes in a single point of space and time. Imagine knowledge knowing how to guide time's moves within all dimensions of time and across all dimensions of space. That could be seen as the ratio operating all of time's changes.

Time moves and conducts by means of the ratio: the equation specifying the speed and direction that shape the conducting. To move is to go at a rate of speed in a particular direction. Without knowing which direction to go, movement will not start. In that sense, the ratio is the knowledge that time needs to move. And this movement is no simple 'from/to' two-step. It appears to be a complex dance in all directions, dimensions, and depths 'at once'.

The ratio connects 'from' and 'to', articulating the baseline and movement along it. Its equations specify all types of motions, rotations, and vibrations. Creating distinctions, it allows knowledge to draw a line in time, whether between two points in space, two particles, two theories, two countries, or two individuals. The ratio gives to the point the holding power that it needs to manifest—the order, rhythm, and transitions essential to be.

OPENING ALL POINTS

If every zero-point sphere of space and time is edgeless and boundless, then every point is infinite, and so is every line of points. Every line defining the edges of the cones is composed of zeros, each replete with 16. But if the line connecting 'from' and 'to' is not solid, the zero face of every cone can be condensed into the zero at the starting point. The background no longer operates. All is space and time.

Even if we add countless degrees of rotation and motion, such a vision cannot be completely specified in three-dimensional time and space. We seem to have hit the limit, to have lost all perspective! Yet nothing is lost. Perspective is just perspective, a way to see and a seeing-through. What does it matter if mind cannot visualize it, if logic cannot delineate it, if words cannot pin it down? Such a prospect is an invitation to train the mind to work in different dimensions, to connect to depths and heights, to angles and horizons that are currently out of reach.

If we are sure that space is space, then space is the zero-point and the zero is space. 'Space-wise', there is no difference between points. If we are sure that time is time, wherever it may be acting, then what is the difference 'time-wise' between points? All points in time are connected, *because* they are time. All points are infused with time's momentum, its dynamic power to change, to transform, to make transitions.

LOOSENING AND UNFOLDING

W e usually imagine that time has been running a long time. Some points in time are older and some are younger. The oldest point of all is the grandfather starting point, Old Zero. Though he was smaller than we can imagine, somehow he was more powerful than anyone around today. All the new points in time are feeble in comparison.

What a strange story to tell! Doesn't it seem more likely that the distinction between Old Zero and new zeros is created by moves of time and knowledge in space? How else do we divide old from new? The prevailing logic says the old ones are farther away, on down the long road of time, back toward the beginning of the beginning. But we have asked before and can ask again: Are all starting points in time somewhere else, not 'now' but 'then'?

Time reminds us: "Without 'from', you cannot have 'to'. Without 'to' you cannot have 'from'. Without 'now' you cannot have 'then'. Without 'then', you cannot have 'now'."

If each zero-point 'here' and 'now' is space and time, it is connected to all points 'then' and 'there'. Points unfold in all directions. If any point in any direction or dimension could be a starting point, 'here' could be 'from' or 'to'.

How could space and time unfold freely if all the directions, dimensions, and ratios of time and space were not present in every point? 16s everywhere means starting points everywhere. Imagine all cones opening up, unfolding or unrolling—boundless space and time in all directions. How could there be more time here and less time over there? How could there be old zero-points and new zero-points?

Space and time say: "All points in time are time and all points in space are space. If there were any unoccupied space and time, points deficient in space or time, then it would matter which point was which. But how could there be a difference between points?"

If each point is a starting point of time and space, history is a story told by the knowledge that belongs to time. If all points are directly and immediately time and space, no one point is privileged over another. The center is everywhere.

There is no way to point out the center of a sphere without an edge. No matter where we cut the endless sphere of space-time, we are still in the center.

Imagine each point is being-time and being-space, fully endowed, completely initiated, and empowered to play out the fundamental ratios of existence. How would it be possible for any point worthy of manifesting time, powerful enough 'to be in time' not to be a complete and perfect representative of being-time? For what are we looking at? Not points located on past-present-future triangles, not slices of flattened time, but being-points of magnificent TIME.

POSITIONING IN TIME

R ationality likes a starting point, so that a good story can be told. That way, details can be aligned along the edges of a single cone, which thinking and minding can track as history. Each point, however, is not one, but 16 in all directions. Space and time are not limited by rules and guidelines established by fiat in the kingdom of logic. Space and time are prior to logic, who is just the great-great-grandson of an ancient union. Even 'prior to' and 'ancient' are concessions to Young Rational, son of Ratio, who wants to know who his parents are and where they came from. From the perspective of the rational, the questions come with great insistence: "How could I be here now if I have no 'then' and 'there'? How could I exist without 'to' and 'from'?" How! Who! Hey! Ho!

Imagine identifying the ancient parental point 'back there' somewhere. "Here it comes! Here comes the whole universe!" exclaims Young Rational in great excitement. But 'here' and 'there' are space-perspectives, as 'now' and 'then' are time-perspectives. They are results of ratios in operation.

Each starting point is 'to' *and* 'from'. If it were otherwise, time and space would not unfold. 'Here' can be 'to'. 'There' can be 'from', 'from' can be 'to', and 'here' can be 'there'. Which is where? It all depends on where we are.

Holding onto our position as the audience, we find ourselves kicked out onto the mean streets of lower-level time and space. We beg for knowledge, but we can receive only the knowledge that fits in our bowl! Sliding down the long linear slope of ordinary time-space-knowledge, we let the point slip away. Secretly, we proclaim: "Time has run out. There are no more starting points to be found."

If time is truly the magnificent time of zero, 16, and ratios, none of this holds up. How could we establish a boundary demarcating the ancient starting-point of the universe from the present moment? What cone extends 'from' that one 'then' 'to' this one 'now' that cannot be unwound into the boundless dynamics of time? What points line up from 'here' to 'there' that cannot be opened up to zero? What position is there that cannot be comprehended as a distinction-making of time itself, a transitioning created by time, the result of a being-time ratio? As positions come unglued, as cones unfurl and baselines telescope to points, we need not fear going over the edge, for we cannot depart from time. We are bonded with time and space, united with all existence in a precise unboundedness.

Following time as a one-way stream, we see only one possible cone of development, and we operate with only a few dimensions of space, time, and knowledge. But if knowledge knows how to operate the ratios, every transition is a new chance. Every change in history, every fleeting moment is testimony to the grand flexibility and transforming power of time. We are point and baseline. We are connected to all zeros and all 16s.

MEETING POINTS

T ime says: "My nature is aliveness that never stops. My action intervenes everywhere, all at once, and all the time. Space allows my rhythms free reign to play out pervasively in all directions."

Zero says: "How could 16 be a one-time happening, an explosion in the past? It is happening now, in all directions and with the full cooperation of all!"

Imagine that within each step of the series that unfolds from 1 to 16 are more transitions. Start with a nanosecond and divide it into 16. To get from 1 to 2, 16 transitions. To get from 2 to 3, another 16. Everywhere, all at once, and all the time. Connections must be made at very precise, minute levels of time, space, and knowledge. And so they are.

Suppose 16s must interact to function at all; that to make the transition, there must be more than one. 16s meet at 15. If a partner does not show up, then 16 cannot hold.

Imagine one zero on the left and one on the right, dancing together to reach completion. A charge flows between them, granting momentum, vibration, and direction. They move, but not from 'here' to 'there'.

How can time and space make a point? Imagine again an image used above: a mirror image of a mirror reflecting a mirror image of another mirror. The images cannot be separated, so there is no way of saying which is the producer. From this union, the point shines forth. The shining is shared via space and time transition. Form can manifest, exist, be known.

The 16th of space and 16th of time share the 16th. Each point is a mirror image of a mirror image of a mirror image, translucent, interpenetrating, reflections of each other, the perfect marriage.

SHARING AND ALLOWING

At the borderline between points, time shares with space and space shares with time. They reflect the image of an image. The mirror image makes the line, builds the foundation, initiates the momentum. But no borders are erected, no walls built. Time does not do anything, but there is sharing. There are parts, fractions, reflections; there are unique units.

Imagine 4x4 sharing a 16th. One connects to another, each linked, protected. With no partition between them, time and space share the unit: 4 points on each side, 4 sides to each point, 4 dimensions, 4 16s.

Can time-space-knowledge truly fit so much in and around and below a single zero-point? Imagine people standing here and there on continents around the earth. There is no below and behind. Everyone is upright from his own point of view. There is plenty of room to connect. When the nanosecond opens up again and again, there is enough time too. Faster than the speed of light is the motion of time.

How deep does this go? Although the nature of the 16th is to make a point, there is no one single way to do so. There might be 16s above and below and to the sides, working together. The connections may be hard to specify, but so are the distinctions. Where does zero end? Where is the borderline?

Space allows borders, but zero's inside and zero's outside may not be different. In the end, top and bottom, betweens and borders cannot be completely defined. The unity and finity of space and time are simply too allowing, too dynamic.

Space and time are so open, so subtle, so precise; the points are so small. There is no wall left, no substance remaining. But 'here' is a starting point. A unit makes a point. Each one shares: 16. . . 16 . . . 16 . . . 16. Space and time build walls made of zero-points and transitions. No distance between, not moving far away, never completely finished. The unit is a point, the point becomes space, and space is unified.

From time to time, space may show different personalities, each with its own features and ways of behaving. Sometimes pregnant, sometimes giving birth, sometimes not yet courted. But time never deserts space or abandons his children.

Time moves in every direction within the cone, within all cones; not confined to the axes, the baseline, the timeline, the chain between subject and object. Time is everywhere time, not bound by here to there, past, present, or future. Not going anywhere, it is pervasive and penetrating. Activating existence in all directions, uniting everything in all reflections, finding birth and death in all the same places, time leaves nothing static, nothing stagnant. Being is alive with time.

Knowledge

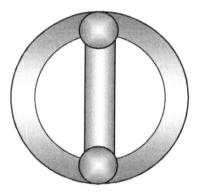

Search for Knowledge

Human beings naturally seek knowledge. We want to know what we can make of our lives, how we can do better, contribute more, or find greater enjoyment. We want to know our origins and our ends, understand how our present circumstances were initiated, find creative solutions to our difficulties, and predict the consequences of our actions. In terms of time, we want to know our history, see our path, and carve our destiny.

History shows us that new knowledge emerges in every age and every circumstance. We are always finding different ways to do things, coming up with innovative ideas, expressing our insights in magnificent and wholly original forms. Sometimes new kinds of knowledge actually open whole dimensions of understanding that were previously unknown. For instance, computers are making us familiar with the notion of cyberspace, which may eventually allow us to rethink the meaning of space itself.

Sometimes, however, an advance in knowledge on one level can actually lead to a loss of knowledge in other dimensions. We think we are making progress, but by some measures we are losing ground. This risk is especially real in times like our own, when change is coming so rapidly that we can suffer serious setbacks before we even realize what is at stake.

Another danger comes when we let ourselves imagine that our specific values and understandings are right, and that we have nothing to learn from others. For instance, most traditional cultures follow rhythms very different from our own, and we tend to assume that we know more than they do. But perhaps it is just that the knowledge they cultivate—through techniques such as meditation, attunement to natural cycles, or the patient exploration of certain kinds of experience—is not so easy for an outsider to observe or appreciate. By dismissing these alternative forms of knowledge, we risk impoverishing our capacities for knowing.

It is natural to assume that our basic orientation to the world—our sense of what is real and who we are, of how events in time unfold and how to acquire knowledge—is established beyond all possibility of questioning. But a brief look at history suggests otherwise. Much of the 'knowledge' that everyone took for granted two centuries ago has been rejected today. We view the world in scientific terms and also see our role as human beings differently. Our sense of morality, our relationship to the physical world, our vision of human destiny: All this has been completely transformed in just a few short generations.

TAKING TIME AND SPACE FOR GRANTED

One element that has changed dramatically in recent times is the nature of change itself. Time seems to be speeding up, and space seems more densely packed. We have learned a great deal about patterns of duplication and mindless replication, which lead to amazing productivity when applied to inanimate objects, but also bring about a pervasive sense of emptiness and boredom in the lives of individuals.

When everything moves so quickly, we are constantly pressured; what is more, we have no time to think about how things might be different than they actually are. Reflection is squeezed out, fantasies multiply, and caring cannot take hold. As momentum builds, our priorities shift; faced with trends whose power seems overwhelming, we adopt a defensive stance toward what the future will bring, and focus more and more on carving out limited domains where we can feel in control of our lives.

In reflecting on the increasing momentum of time, we might wonder whether time itself has not changed its qualities. But that is the kind of question that gives us trouble. We have learned to think of time as fixed and invariable, even though we know that our subjective experience of time is always in flux. For us, time is tied to the regular rhythms of specific physical processes, from the sun rising and setting to the vibrations of atoms. Like space, it is a given, a framework for experience that we feel we can safely ignore.

We might see this 'taking for granted' as a warning sign. Time—and space—are fundamentals. If our aim is to improve our knowledge, going to the fundamentals may be our best strategy. How does knowledge interact with time and space? Does it know them directly? Can it affect them? How do their dynamic and presence affect its possibilities?

When time and space are understood to be fixed and absolute, we should not be too surprised if we sometimes feel that things are out of control, that our destiny is not in our hands. Our society cherishes human freedom, but in some ways the ratio of freedom to determinism seems to have tilted toward determinism. Though we assert our claims of autonomy, our choices unfold within an increasingly narrow arena, beyond whose bounds overwhelming forces may be gathering.

PROBLEMATICS OF KNOWLEDGE

Caught up in time, we are rushing through our lives like someone strapped to a board floating down a broad and powerful river. But knowledge can question this way of being. Board and river are parts and points. Different alternatives must be available, different rhythms and different transitions, differently allowed by time and space.

When one point appears, it seems there are automatically others. But how did we arrive at the first point? Where are we now, how did we get here, and where are we headed? What are we losing and what are we gaining? What kinds of developments have there been over time? What are the ratios that shape this circumstance: those that existed in the past, those that might exist in the future, and those that could never exist at all?

These questions seem to make sense, but our ways of dealing with them are limited. We see ourselves playing the role of the one who knows, and as knowers we know by applying a certain set of tools, including presuppositions and fixed methodologies. We understand with an 'according to' understanding.

Suppose, however, that knowledge revealed itself differently: not 'according to' this or that structure, but so directly that there was no one for it to reveal itself *to*. This would mean departing from measurability, with its distinctions and divisions. Would knowledge be diminished? Or would knowledge be enthroned: master, friend, and lover of time and space?

As the one who knows, the subjective knower, we are concerned with finding new 'sources' of knowledge. We devote ourselves to 'figuring out' how to connect pre-established points, increase what is already in operation, and make progress along predetermined lines. Patterns we cannot release preoccupy all alternatives. We set up housekeeping in the confined realm of the point we have occupied, the 'here' from which we look out on every possible 'there'. The point may have the capacity to open to a deeper being, but this point-being has been lost.

Imagine that time-space-knowledge are like a phonograph record playing on a turntable. To live in the point that subjective knowledge offers is a little like being a bug making its way across the surface of the record, loyal only to the rhythms of its own movement.

Suppose we approach this bug, expressing our sympathy for the hard work its efforts to move 'forward' require. We fall into conversation, and at some point we suggest that there might be another way. The bug draws back, suddenly suspicious. "I don't like living like this, but I don't have a choice!" If we persist, the bug grows angry. "How dare you!" it tells us. And indeed, we have been impolite. We might think of the bug as a lifelong mourner at its own funeral: Who would have the poor taste to tell it no one has died?

Yet the bug has a point. How is it—how are we—to change? If change is not possible, it seems unfair even to bring it up. But in that case we have no choice. We wake up from our dream of knowledge to find ourselves in the business of selling limitations, with a brand new shipment of goods already lining our shelves. Sales are brisk, and money pours into our cash register, but somehow our standard of living never improves, and we can never take a day off. The reason is simple: We are our only customer, and we buy compulsively, because there is nothing else for sale.

QUESTIONING OUR COMMITMENTS

Is mind truly so limited, its creativity confined to such a narrow domain? Must it rely on the cycles of sameness, turning assumptions and rumors into established history? The long and painful record of human suffering, largely unchanged down through centuries, might seem to support this grim conclusion, but there are also alternatives. We know that new knowledge is possible; we know that there have been individuals of great genius and inspiration who advanced human understanding immeasurably. Can their efforts and insights inspire our own?

One alternative to the standard ways of knowing is speculation. Even sheer flights of fantasy may be helpful if they allow us to break through the presupposed. But can we be sure that our speculations will not lead us into delusion? Only if we are confident that knowledge is fundamentally trustworthy. If we want to be clear on that point, the best approach is to test knowledge out. When we exercise our capacity to know, what happens? What are the results?

In exercising knowledge, it seems we can start anywhere, even with the wildest fairy tales. The only danger would be that we would reach a fixed conclusion too early in our inquiry. If we grow convinced that we have arrived at the truth, distinctions and divisions are inevitable: "I understand, but you do not; I am not, but you are!"

Why not aim at a precision that does not turn into rigid positions? When knowledge leads us toward inspiration, we retain the intelligence to recognize the risk of dogma. We see how people build altars to their own private gods, their own unquestionables, accepting the commandments they issue. Perhaps we even see such tendencies operating in ourselves.

OPENING THE POINT

Ordinary knowledge depends on making the point. The starting point is the observer, the one who knows. But the point is also to know the object, and it is also the object known. The knowledge pointer moves from point to point, going round the 360 degrees of a circle, specifying first this, then that. Perceptions and thoughts lead to shapes and forms, and these in turn lead to meanings, distinctions, associations, and conclusions. In this way the point is made.

In making the point, knowledge relies on space and time. We can see in our own experience that different kinds of thoughts and perceptions engage space and time differently. Clarity, confusion, indifference, passion, anger: Each has its kind of time, measured out along such dimensions as momentum, intensity, pressure, and speed; and each also has its own space, measured in terms such as density, congruence, degrees of structure, and tightness. Watching the patterns of mind unfolding, we can see these qualities shifting from day to day or moment to moment, and operating differently in the various parts of our lives.

More fundamental than these variations are the structures of time and space inherent in a way of knowing that proceeds from point to point. For such a knowing, points proliferate fast and furious, far too quickly to take note of. The circle or sphere that marks out the potential range of experience is always thickly filled with branching possibilities and overlapping cones. Caught in this dense thicket, knowledge circles round and round, repeating itself, like a bee flying back and forth from one flower to the next. Its patterns generate their own momentum, which easily begins to accelerate, going out of control.

We have grown used to such an inner enviroment, but if we imagine looking at it from a fresh perspective, we would have to say that it seemed unhealthy. It is as though we were steadily running a low-grade fever. Yet the momentum seems too firmly established to turn it in a different direction. Knowledge has no way to rest and restore itself, no way to allow for healing.

Still, the whole of this structure is based on the point of knowledge. If we knew how to open each point as it arose, there would be no opportunity for the momentum of the whole to develop. The effect on our well-being, our sense of being at home in the world, could be enormous. And at the same time, the way might be open for different forms of knowledge to develop.

To open the point of knowledge, we would have to recognize it as the zero-point. At the very beginning of conventional, first-level knowledge, the zero-point is available—the prior of perception. To return to that point is to engage the openness of space, to accommodate experience differently.

As an analogy for what this might mean, we might think of relaxing at the end of a difficult day, letting gentle music heal the tension that has accumulated in our bodies and mind. Gradually, the mind begins to move along a different track, allowing the senses to renew their contact with experience. The focal setting shifts, and perception deepens. At a subtle level, knowledge begins to heal itself from the damage inflicted by a point-centered way of knowing.

Opening the point might have this same flavor. But if it is to make a real difference in the way we engage knowledge, such an opening will have to operate in the midst of our ordinary knowing, not just when we withdraw from our usual activities. Does that seem possible?

The starting point of knowledge is the knower, the 'I' of 'I am here'. Can we open that point? How would we begin, without immediately turning that beginning into another starting point?

How do we pursue *this* question? If we immediately set out to make the point, we will find ourselves caught up in first-level structures. Can we allow instead for a different, zero-based kind of knowing? Rather than always looking straight ahead, can we open the angle of awareness, the cone that radiates from the point? Can we allow for vision that sees in all directions? Even though the inquiry proceeds in abstract terms, can we let it be guided by what actually happens in the process of inquiry?

IGNORING TIME AND SPACE

Knowledge brings order into our experience. But what is the order that governs the arising of knowledge itself? In asking this question, we know at the outset that knowledge accumulates in time. Not only does knowledge build up from one generation to the next, but in our own lives we grow in knowledge as we grow to maturity. And even when we set out to increase our knowledge right now, we expect that this process will take time and develop in time. For all these reasons, it seems to make sense to start with the cone of time as a model for how knowing arises.

Perhaps our most basic assumption about knowledge is that it starts off as the property of an individual knower. If we consider a knower engaged in an act of knowing, what is the temporal cone that leads to that particular event? Actually, there seem to be several, all terminating at the same point. There is the cone of events in the knower's personal life that have led up to the moment of observation, the cone of mental operations that immediately precede the act of knowing and make it possible, and the cone of historical events that create the circumstances and conditions that frame the particular act of knowing. We can readily confirm the operation of these cones in our own knowledge activity, seeing how they interact, and finding others as well.

Once we have accounted for the knower, we still have to consider the act of knowing. Here we might imagine another cone, radiating out from the knower at the apex like a beam of light, illuminating the object of inquiry at the base of the cone. The particular qualities of this cone would vary in accord with the shaping cones of time that have influenced the knower.

For instance, we could imagine that each of the knowledge disciplines developed by human beings relies on its own cone of knowledge, shaped in characteristic ways and disclosing characteristic events. As the light of these different cones radiates out, they disclose very different truths, some beautiful, others frightening, chaotic, or inspiring, still others routine and readily predictable.

Thus, if we know through the cone of knowledge that emerges from a religious orientation, we may discover a world governed by divine purpose and infused by ties that bind human beings to their creator— a reality that imposes duties and obligations and offers protection and ultimately salvation. If we use the cone developed in certain philosophies, the world we see will reveal a destiny for human beings in relation to the cosmos. The cone of science will disclose a world that obeys fundamental mathematical rules.

No matter what specific form a cone of knowledge takes, it seems to share with every other cone a basic structure. The object (or field) of inquiry is located somewhere else, at the other end of the cone. The axis of the cone defines the distance between knower and known, serving as the baseline that separates 'here' (where the knower is located) from 'there'.

The 'here/there' structure of the cone depends on both time and space, for 'there' is separated from 'here' both temporally and physically. Even for objects that are immediately present (for instance, a vase on the table in front of me), the act of knowing takes a measurable amount of time and crosses over a measurable amount of space.

Busy with the task of acquiring useful information, knowledge does its best to ignore space and time. The distance between subject and object is a barrier, and space and time, which construct the barrier, are *obstacles*. Lower-level knowledge either admits the obstacle, ignores it, or tries to account for it in order to set it aside. Under these conditions, the idea that space and time themselves could be the key to a different, transforming knowledge rarely arises or gains momentum.

At the base of this strained relationship between knowledge and time and space, certain assumptions operate: Space has its three dimensions, time has the tripartite structure of past, present, and future, and knowledge is the property of an observer. Suppose these characteristics changed. Would time and space cease to be obstacles to knowledge? Could they perhaps become its friends and supporters? Would the knowledge cone collapse, to be replaced by some other structure? Or would the cone itself be transformed, opening to reveal new dimensions?

ACTIVATING TIME AND SPACE

It is usually argued that even if time and space could function differently, human knowledge could not become aware of this difference. For instance, if space had four dimensions rather than three, we could not visualize objects that occupied all four dimensions, nor could we inhabit the fourth dimension ourselves. If time were somehow timeless, or if past, present, and future could be united, we would have no way to appreciate or bring about this change.

Yet the relationship between knowledge and time or space may not be quite this firmly fixed. To see for ourselves, we might try visualizing a cone of knowledge in operation in each single act of knowing. In this way we would turn from an exclusive preoccupation with the object of knowledge and become aware of the subject together with the object. Perhaps this single change would already be enough to make time and space available somewhat differently.

By turning to the cone of knowledge, we would also have the chance to notice the dynamics and the structures that link subject and object together, whether these operate in time, in space, or in knowledge. Do such structures operate differently depending on whether we are focusing on thoughts and images or physical sensations? Do time and space operate differently in the mental and physical realms? Is it fair to speak of space in the context of mental operations?

Looking toward the cone of knowledge in this way discloses new objects of inquiry, and may expand the potential range of knowledge. But for now, the main point is that by conducting this exercise, we seem to activate automatically a different appreciation for the time and space that operate the distance of the cone. And this simple appreciation in turn brings new clarity and aliveness to the knowing act. It is as though space were more richly available and time more dynamically charged.

The moment we find ways to let knowledge turn toward time and space, time and space themselves seem to change their personalities, becoming more accommodating and alive. In turn knowledge becomes more open to the fullness of the situation it is engaging. Could we encourage these tendencies? Are there ways for knowledge to engage space and time more directly— to take on a time and space embodiment?

Structures
of Knowledge

W hen knowledge treats time and space as shaping structures and tools for measurement, it finds itself operating in a highly patterned and routinized world. Once the baseline of the cone has given 'from' and 'to', appearance is determined almost exclusively by what can be measured out and identified. With derivation, difference, and distinctions central, it is not surprising that limits on knowledge show up. Certain problems prove insoluble; certain areas of inquiry (for example, what will happen in the future) are out of bounds.

Against the grid of empty space and measured-out time, a universe of solid objects takes form. As notions and assumptions grow ever more concrete, decisions as to right and wrong and true and false are made, and the self takes up its role as knower and doer. Projections and juxtapositions emerge from the already established, limiting what can manifest in the future. The ratio of knowledge to ignorance is fixed, and knowledge can only abide by that ratio, searching for the clues that will help it make decisions, establish values, and work out possibilities. The world that emerges from these structures is endlessly rich in appearances and phenomena, but it is also often confusing and chaotic, frustrating and even hostile.

All this seems natural to us, almost self-evident. But is our picture accurate? Present awareness projects a realm of space (the universe and the objects in it) and a realm of time (life and experience). But if time and space themselves are ignored and taken for granted, are these projections trustworthy? For instance, does space really operate in only three dimensions? Does time really move only from past to present to future? If space and time are different, could knowledge project itself forward differently?

One of the hardest things for lower-level knowledge to do is to notice its own limits. Yet if we begin to suspect that time and space could be different, we can at least imagine that knowledge would be different also. Each moment, we are reacting to what time presents and space allows. What if the full range of this presenting has been cut off by our restricted view of time and space? What if the knowledge we have learned to trust and rely on has been steering us away from a greater knowledgeability that is spontaneously and directly available?

At present we may not know how that can be. But perhaps we can let the quality of yearning, the suspicion that we are the victims of a very great loss, rise up in our hearts. Such feelings can support our inquiry.

When we think we know, when we decide we understand, is the yearning for deeper, more fulfilling knowledge still close at hand? If so, our claim may not need to be investigated further. The testimony of such feelings suggests that we have not yet gone far enough; that hidden limits to our knowledge are at work.

FROM AND NOT-FROM

From/to' and the 'here/there' baseline are the foundation for our first-level understanding of space-time dimensionality. Every cone of knowledge has its point of origin in the knower. Situated 'here', the knower reaches out to an object of inquiry that is situated 'there'; i.e., at some distance in space and time. The knower, the known, time, and space are all given together, all interdependent.

This structure dominates our way of making sense of the world. It allows for certain kinds of experience, which can only manifest in time in limited ways. It permits a certain understanding of substance, which can only appear in space in limited ways. And it establishes a certain understanding of the self as knower, only able to know in limited ways.

Substance, experience, and self-as-knower all share the same understanding of time and space. There is no point in challenging any one of them without challenging the others. This may seem almost impossible, since we must always mount our challenge from a point within the pre-established time-space-knowledge structure. But perhaps we have not been framing our questions at the right level.

Suppose that knowledge did not start out from the point of origin and thus did not establish a 'from' or a baseline. Suppose it did not construct a history at all. With no baseline, there would be no distance, and this would free space and time from having to play their accustomed roles as distance-makers. Could time and space appear differently? Could they open new possibilities for experience, substance, and the self as knower?

If the present point of origin was just another point, no different from a point on the other side of the universe—or even several universes removed—how could mind rely on its usual compass or build from its usual blueprint? What would become of directions in space or time, of 'up' and 'down' or 'now' and 'then'? Without directions, would there still be a foundation for knowledge? If not, would this mean a fall into ignorance? Or would it perhaps mean that a knowledge not consistent with 'from' and 'to'—a knowledge that was not the property of a knower—could at last emerge?

SUBJECTIVITY OF FROM

In ordinary experience, mind sets out before we know it. A thought pops up, seemingly from nowhere. From this origin, a momentum manifests: Mind moves toward what is already known as if drawn by a magnet. Word and image arise, and together shape appearance.

At this point, well before conscious recognition and response, the cone of knowledge has taken form. Already we are situated 'here', at a point defined by the axes; already we direct our attention somewhere else, down the baseline of the cone; already we have turned time and space into abstract yardsticks for measuring the distance that separates us from the world of objects.

We may look on this model with approval, because it seems calculated to give us 'objective' knowledge. But the analogy with the well-defined forms and principles of geometry is misleading. A set of axes in mathematical terms is nothing but a measuring device. But in the geometry of our lives, any point comes into being through a complex history. Situated 'here', we are subject to certain pressures and tensions created by previous conditions and circumstances. For instance, the initial point and baseline of 'I am here' respond to the need of the self to assert its own existence. From a knowledge perspective, the emerging zero-point of knowledge that the self claims as its own is strongly determined by the need to be right, to have things under control.

As a way of exploring these limits on our knowledge, we might imagine that the pre-existing tensions that contribute to the origin of the zero-point deform the axes that situate the 'here'. If the axes moved out of the perpendicular; if the angle of their intersection shifted, could we tell the difference? What would it mean in experiential terms for such distortion to occur? Could we trace the consequences? Could we detect the flavor of such distortion in the characteristic 'feel' of the knowledge with which we operate? Are there domains of knowledge in which we notice this flavor more strongly? Are there others where it disappears?

Even if the axes of the zero-point are not distorted, once the zero, the axes, and the baseline have been established, other forces of distortion come into play. We might imagine that a kind of gravity begins to exert its pull. In the very first nanoseconds, a steady stream of adjustments is already shaping the point and its axes, giving rise to an ever shifting ratio of interacting elements. Constant transitions are required to maintain the point in balance.

Point of Access

S uppose we reduced the whole world to a single point. As a meeting point for time and space, that single point would also be an access point for knowledge. But the moment we treat the point as a point of origin, we close that access off. The point of origin becomes a 'from', the 'here' for a knower who can only find knowledge 'there'. We find ourselves pursuing the endless repetitions and variations that radiate out from the point of origin. We move forward and backward, inside and out, never really getting anywhere. If we ask for the real, we affirm our limits; if we arrive at the notion 'not real', we are still confirming what is so.

When we trace knowledge to a starting point, the cone of knowledge is also the cone of existence. The time-space baseline situates in a way that determines and makes real. It establishes and discloses a world that seems solid in every respect.

We do seem to have another choice. Understanding this emerging structure, reflecting on its presuppositions and tracing its dynamic in our own experience, allows a different kind of knowledge to emerge. We can recognize how 'from/to' interactions put together the reality in which we operate. We can become more sensitive to the process through which we know and name, and less bound to the outcome of that process. We can learn to identify the tensions that shape the seemingly innocent structures of subjective knowledge.

As an exercise in developing this kind of knowledge, we might try exploring in our own thoughts the styles of knowing employed in various disciplines and fields, or at various times among different cultures. It might be especially helpful to focus on those with which we are familiar through our own education and training, but we could also try to make an imaginative leap to other fields and disciplines and other styles of knowledge. Perhaps we could look at those used by friends or colleagues, trying to recognize the underlying structures. Looking at styles and approaches where we sense a strong conflict with our own approach could be especially helpful.

In experimenting in this way, one good place to look is at the tendency in every field to absolutize the methods and premises that operate there. But it may be even more important to appreciate the different dynamics and structures that knowledge can shape and inhabit. In that way, we may be able to see more clearly our own absolutizing tendencies at work.

The prospect of developing this kind of knowledge suggests that we may be able to move a step or two away from the rigid, fixed limits of the 'from/to' structure. If we sense some degree of opening, we could test it out by turning to the problem areas of our lives and seeing whether we can explore them differently. For instance, we may find within one point of confusion patterns that link it to every other point of confusion. Questioning these patterns and their assumptions and presuppositions, we may be able to penetrate obstacles that formerly seemed solid, or to discover limiting patterns where before everything seemed transparent. Seeing, we can predict; having predicted, we can transform. Liberating knowledge from the rigid structures we formerly adopted, we may eventually be able to open a realm of ultimate value, letting it flower in our own lives and sharing it with others.

Opening Knowledge

There are many paths to knowledge that rely on 'from': disciplines such as religion, science, or philosophy, the study of patterns at the social level or patterns in language, inquiry into self-image or the deeper levels of the personality. But because such schools of thought and modes of inquiry accept the structure of the baseline, the range of their investigations is fixed in advance. As they establish their subject matter and implement their approach, they are affirming a fundamental limit on knowledge, rooted in the particular structuring of time and space that the baseline imposes.

In taking this approach to knowledge, we can certainly accumulate valuable information and develop useful techniques. We can also build theories and similar structures of great beauty, and open to the wonder and excitement that knowledge offers. Yet if we think of the basic questions that arise for us as human beings, the limits of this style of inquiry make it likely that in the end we will be frustrated. We are like a traveler knocking on the door of a strange house, hoping to gain entry. Not only does the door never open, but we find ourselves wondering again and again if we have been knocking at the wrong house.

And indeed, it may be so. We direct our attention toward concrete existence. What of the space and time that make existence possible? Why not focus the search for knowledge there?

Orders
of Knowledge

As human beings, we seem unique in our capacity to look back, to make sense, to give meaning to the idea of destiny. But even though we embody knowledge, are we really so sure that we are its source?

The self insists on its own being, and on its role as the one who imposes order on the play of events and appearance in time and space. Suppose we could take the whole universe and roll it up into a giant, hollow tube. We can be sure that immediately the entire tube would be filled with the claims of the self, with an "I am here" leading to an "I know this!"

The self makes the structure of the 'from' its own. It propagates forward the constructs it claims to have established, including the construct of its own existence. But we have reason to be suspicious. Again and again the order the self imposes breaks down; again and again it must be reconfigured and reconfirmed. The self takes this burden on willingly, for in this way it confirms its own central role. But why must it be this way? Why does the structure prove inherently unstable?

SOURCES OF INCOMPLETENESS

S ighting down the cone of knowledge, the subject perceives the world as object. Subject and object stand opposed—at opposite ends of the cone—but they are also partners. Their mutual connection establishes the baseline along which the 'from' of the cone unfolds. Along this baseline, different kinds of relationships can take form: perception, sensation, ownership, appropriation, love, contemplation, and so on.

Usually we understand these relationships solely from the perspective of the subject, which knows with the mind. The mind connects to this, produces that, cognizes something else: It reacts to what appears before it, assigns shape and form, sponsors and directs, and makes use of. It produces stories and explanations that accumulate into histories and compelling accounts. Yet this way of looking seems one-sided. The subject imposes order, but the materials of the objective world must be open for such order to be imposed. The subject may be the active partner, but the world is the silent partner, providing the capital. The partnership is equal.

Interacting with the world of objects, the subject builds up knowledge. But such a knowledge, based on the 'from', is always sealed off from the object by distance in time and space. The subjective knower must

166

rely on the data of perception to bridge the gap between 'here' and 'there', 'now' and 'then'.

Intent on transforming the obscure into the certain, the knower recalls and readjusts, reformulates and re-orders. To confirm its results, it relies on repeatability, predictability, and objectifiability. Yet in all of this, knowledge can only proceed indirectly. The time-space distance between knower and known cannot be bridged.

The result is a kind of cognitive friction or interference. As the identity and characteristics of both the subject and object grow more and more complex, communication breaks down. Obscurities emerge: mysteries and uncertainties, misinterpretations and false expectations, contradictions and blind spots. Some are so subtle that we fail to see them, but others are the stuff of our lives: disappointment, confusion, lack of clarity, and emotionality. With a distanced form of knowledge in operation, nothing is truly certain, nothing wholly reliable.

DISTANCING THROUGH LANGUAGE

The structures of the 'from' are faithfully preserved, and even augmented, in the naming activity of language. Language is abstract, in the literal sense that it abstracts from being, so how can it hold the full meaning? As language names, it introduces a presupposed familiarity with what is identified, a ratio of the new to the old. But a second ratio is also established: the gap between being and the words we use to name it. Shaped by these ratios, knowledge cannot arrive at the heart of what is named. And because language is directed outward in the act of naming, the inner lines of its own development, which might give access to a more immediate knowing, are almost always hidden from view.

For instance, we have called the point of origin for the cone of knowledge the 'zero-point'. In offering us this possibility, language discloses a potential for new knowledge. In fact, it is the abstracting power of language that gives us this opening into time and space, for no one would suggest that the point is physically zero, or that 'zero' as it is understood at the physical level of appearance can be linked to our own being. Yet the moment we name the zero-point, we depart from zero. In naming, we situate. We affirm the distance between knower and known, and at once we are on the way to establishing something solid.

It is not easy to 'take hold' of zero without relying on language. But if we let zero resonate within our experience, reflecting on existence and non-existence and on how these both relate to zero, we may be able to arrive at some understanding that is not just based on language.

In such an inquiry, the thought arises that 'within' zero, distance does not operate. Let us assume that to be so. In that case, to speak of zero is to use language against itself, naming what resists naming. We might say that this is a way of playing with language, but we might also question whether we are pushing language too far. Are we just bluffing? Are we just spinning tales for a cold winter's night?

Perhaps so. But if that were the whole story, there would be little point to a book such as this one. We need to remind ourselves that language has another side. Although it names and determines and classifies, it also allows for new meanings and alternative constructs. In this way it can undermine the linear structure that determines the shape of the cone of knowledge. If we want to question language, it may be that our best ally is language itself.

Using language to question what language has set in place, we open a dialogue; we activate something new. We can set the momentum of this exchange against the linear momentum of 'from/to'. Playing these two dynamics against one another, whether by telling stories, describing images, or opening to speculation, we may be able to take a step toward opening the cone— toward freeing time and space from the rigid and confined role that subjective knowledge assigns them.

OPENING THE CONE

What would it be like to open the cone of knowledge, taking apart the baseline and the 'from'? Imagine a cone constructed out of paper, shaped by a seam that has been glued together along the baseline. Now we dissolve the glue, so that the cone uncurls into a flat sheet of paper. With this single motion, the point of origin has vanished!

What is the experience that corresponds to this image? When the cone opens and the 'from' dissolves, have we lost all perspective? Usually we think of a perspective as a point of view, suggesting that it will have a single point at its center. But this definition may also be a matter of perspective. A point of view depends on a framing background, and if the cone opens, the background vanishes. What is the point of view then?

When someone walks down the street, looking at various objects, the point of view is the person's shifting location. But perhaps the perspective could be something more encompassing. Perhaps it could include the setting, the situation, the past and future of each moment and each perception. Perhaps it could engage the whole.

PERSPECTIVE OF THE WHOLE

A perspective of the whole will depend on no particular point, for the whole of the cone has been distributed out among all points and in all directions. Nothing belongs to anyone; no point is established. Structures such as point and axes, 'here' and 'there', 'to' and 'from' present themselves, but we do not have to insist on their coherence or line them up with strict regard to their order.

This new wholeness frees time and space in a fundamental way. In the glued-together cone, the 'glue' seems to be time and space, each of which sustains the distance that 'from' has specified. Now time and space come unstuck. They are available throughout the whole.

And so is knowledge, for it is no longer assigned to the single position of the point of origin.

This freedom reverberates through our being. No longer bound to the linear structure of the cone, we are also freed from the isolation of the point. We can dance from point to point, dancing the wholeness of their space manifestation and the rhythms of their time dynamic.

When we look at our present situation from the perspective of the whole, we discover a different dynamic within the subjective point of view. We realize that we do not have to accept or reject conventional structures, and also do not have to put in place some new version of reality. We did not choose, but we were also not chosen. We did not set up, but we have also not been set up. Whatever operates now is one face of the whole. 'I am here' does not confine us. How can it, when it is simply the front side of zero, the mask through whose mouth we first hear of the point of origin?

The perspective of the whole frees knowledge to look at knowledge. Perhaps we have held on too stubbornly to the models for knowledge our culture has developed and passed on to us. Perhaps we have been too quick to accept a particular point of view and too slow to let space and time speak to us directly. But now that these limitations have been recognized, there is no need to reject the knowledge we have built up until now. Instead, we can look for the knowledge within knowledge. There is the wave, but there is also the curve of the wave. And beyond that, there is the ocean.

When knowledge is open to time and space, it holds open the dynamic of the whole: the quiet ocean depths together with the intricate patterns of waves that ripple across the water's surface. It takes responsibility for an order that does not have to be imposed. In this, what need is there for replacing wrong with right?

When knowledge sees the prevailing ratios and distinctions, knowledge can develop knowledge. Perception can change, time can change, reality can change. An opening presents itself, and within the opening light emerges. Now we have a point of access. First we imagine, then we visualize, then we develop. What else is required?

KNOWLEDGE EVERYWHERE

From an open time-space-knowledge perspective, order appears, but it does not hold. The changes we observe around and within us point to the dynamic wholeness folded within the linear directionality of time. The proliferation of objects suggests the power of space to accommodate without limits. And the shifting values and interpretations that come and go in different cultures, different belief systems, and in our own lives remind us that knowledge operates within each limited perspective.

Is all this only theory, or can we begin to imagine how we might align ourselves with this realization? For instance, can we bring mind and senses into balance, so that each supports the other? Can we give up our focus on predictability and explanation to access the past and future within the present? Can we let knowledge emerge within language and consciousness, without being owned by the speaker and the knower?

Suppose that the power of time to allow transitions and the power of space to accommodate appearance introduce knowledge to form and substance, and that knowledge in turn, by giving to space and time their form, lets the world emerge. In this way of looking, what becomes of the limits the self puts in place?

The more knowledge becomes an expression of the time and space in operation, the less we are tempted to put the self at the center. Perhaps it would help to use a different model. For instance, we might think of time, space, and knowledge as three cylinders turning at the center of our being, each inside the other, each independent but also interacting with the others. Tracing their operation and dynamic, visualizing rays of knowledge, time, and space radiating from this center, we might experience how our energy and our intelligence, our power to bring about change and to preserve what has value, are all shaped by this interplay.

From this perspective, nothing that we do will take us outside time and space and knowledge. When we assign size and shape, or label appearance in accord with the narrow ratios of chemistry or history or geology; when we lose ourselves in a stream of images or abandon our own responsibility to knowledge, choosing instead to foster patterns of replication, we are still engaging time-space interactions, brought to light through the power of knowledge.

NEW BODY OF KNOWLEDGE

If the world we encounter and are part of takes form through ratio, we might call space, time, and knowledge the sponsors of the ratio, letting its transitions manifest. Can we allow that the order that governs this becoming may not be an order we impose? Can we view our own attempt at order as just another 'something' happening? Can we imagine these two orders as operating at different levels and in accord with a different dynamic?

Once this distinction is available to us, it seems natural to say that making the transition from one order to the other may be the best hope for knowledge in our time. If we are the product of the time-space-knowledge exhibition, then we are also inseparable from its source. If we knew this to be so in each nanosecond of our lives, would we embody knowledge differently? Could we give birth to this magical new body of knowledge, rich with the unexpected and the inexplicable? Could we enter the womb of transformation?

Cone of
Knowledge

What is the zero-point for knowledge, the 'from' that originates the knowing act? The most open formulation seems to be that the zero-point of knowledge is 'here', and that what is known is 'there'.

How are 'here' and 'there' connected: What is the nature of the distance between them? In our earlier analysis, we described this distance in terms of time (since it 'takes' time for the act of inquiry to move from here to there) and also space (since here is necessarily separate from there). But distance also seems to be a construct of knowledge itself. It arises when we separate, and also when we take a point of view.

The cone of knowledge that radiates along the baseline between 'here' and 'there' can be seen as setting the limits for the kinds of knowing that the self brings to bear. What is inside the cone is what can be known; what is outside the cone is the inconceivable. However, this only begins to describe the restrictions on knowledge that are in operation. While the cone is a field for knowledge, it is largely inaccessible to knowledge, which is directed exclusively toward the object located 'there'. As an image for this limitation, we might imagine the self sending out its agents (for instance, logic or the senses) along the walls of the cone to gather information about the distant object and report back.

CONES WITHIN CONES

T he limits this image is meant to evoke are well-established and easy to identify. Knowledge is not available in all directions equally, nor is it free from limits we impose. We know in accord with our biases and prejudices, and our knowledge is limited by the tools available to us and the capacities we have learned to develop. A ten-year-old child cannot use careful logic to arrive at a conclusion; a novice in business cannot draw on experience to know what will produce good results; and a seasoned craftsman cannot easily adapt to new technologies developed by a new generation.

How solid are these limits, as expressed in the structure of the cone and its baseline? A cone radiates out along its own lines of directionality, but how are these lines generated? One answer is to say that they are constructs formed through previous acts of knowing, each of which started out from its own 'here'. For each such act of knowing, a different cone has been engaged, so that the surface of the cone we started with is actually made up of countless additional cones. And each of these cones may branch out to other cones. Can we conceive of knowing in a way that stays true to the shape of the initial cone, but at the same time remains open to these endless branchings of knowledge? Would such a way of understanding, unbounded yet highly structured, introduce the factor of creativity into the rigid structure of the cone?

INTERCONNECTIVITY

When we imagine that knowledge arises as we look from the point of origin at the apex of the cone, we are saying that what we know will be confined to the angle of vision that the cone measures out. But the 'here' that constitutes the starting-point of the cone is also a zero-point. It is open to the fullness of 16. Could we return to this fullness? Could knowledge see through a 360 degree range in all dimensions of time and space?

Consider again the time-space cone that we have used as an image for the creation of the universe from a hypothetical 'Big Bang'. Something travels 'from' the point of origin in the past 'to' the future, moving through time and allowing for physical expansion in space. Since we are looking at the whole of the universe, whatever appears in space and time is bound to this same cone, but also exhibits its own particularity. I am different from you, but we are also both related to the cone. The same is true for all existents in all the realms that make up reality: the chemical, the mechanical, and so on; each is different, but each is the same.

In describing the link between sameness and difference, we might say that different logics operate in different realms; possibly even different kinds of time and space. Yet a shared time and space are active as well. Whether we look to the level of atomic structure, chemistry, and biology, or to the very different level of civilization, art, music, government, and social structures, certain shared aspects will operate, making knowledge possible. Depending on our focus, we might describe these shared factors as existence-centered, object-centered, causality-centered, and so on.

This mutuality or interconnectedness of knowledge at the level of existence in time and space is so fundamental that we might easily miss it. Chemicals are connected; language is connected; the senses are connected; the continents are connected; everything that appears at this moment in time is connected. Nothing can be totally isolated.

In addition, there is something like the connectedness of connectivity. For example, the senses and language can both point toward the same thing. What allows for this mutuality?

The self as knower considers itself in some sense unique, 'here' as opposed to 'there'. Yet 'here' is still a part of the universe. When the self takes its perspective or develops a certain understanding, it shares in the 'universal' space-time-knowledge cone.

How does this interconnectivity translate into knowledge terms? It seems that the answer will depend strongly on how knowledge conceives of the space-time structures it participates in. If it accepts those structures as solid; if it commits to the way things are as the defining limit of its capacity, it will be bound to the cone in the ways we have been describing. The inherent fullness of the zero-point will become the structured certainty of the starting point: the 'here' that leads to a pre-established 'there'. The knowledge cone will enter into the distributed reality of the always changing but always interconnected 'cone of the whole'.

On the other hand, if knowledge is not bound to the 'here/there' structure given by the cone of subjective knowledge, it will not be limited in these same ways. Knowledge will simply be knowledge, without restriction or identity. In each act of structuring, each making of each cone, knowledge will be 'here' *and* 'there'; in fact, it will be everywhere. For wherever we identify a cone, wherever we draw on time and space to establish the distance along which the cone unfolds, we are invoking the power of knowledge.

Can such knowledge become directly available? At this point, that possibility may seem remote or abstract. But perhaps the model of the cone can be of help. For instance, what if we return to our earlier exercise of seeing the objects and situations we encounter as the outcome of a cone of knowing? Before, we focused on how time and space operate within the cone, looking to open up the baseline of distance along which the cone unfolds. Now we could look at how knowledge operates to frame each situation in terms of 'here' and 'there'. It is like watching a film without getting caught up in the story, focusing instead on the way the director has chosen to present each scene and construct the whole.

It may also be possible to question more fundamentally. In looking at the structure of the cone of knowledge, we suggested that it could be seen as made up of countless points, each the starting point for an act of knowing. From 'my' perspective 'here', such points cannot serve as starting point, and for this reason subjective knowledge tends to slide past this complexity, looking for a more solid and established 'there'. Yet the points are available, and each of them expresses the fullness of 16. Can we connect to that availability?

Let us do some symbolic mathematics. If each point that goes into the construction of a knowledge cone embodies 16, and each 16 opens into another 16, and so on, what will be the stopping point? Suppose we designate this unfolding structure as 16^{16}. Simple calculation gives more than 18 sextillion interconnections. Perhaps we can see no way right now to enter into those possibilities. But at least we can ask ourselves: If the cone is that open, how can it limit us?

Wandering in this galaxy of alternatives, we might find it appropriate to return to an earlier image, imagining the cone is made of light. Or we may wish to say that the cone, having originated in the fullness of zero, now opens to zero; that each point that figures in its construction becomes the host for infinite perspectives.

Does this image threaten us with the loss of the familiar perspective that keeps the self at the apex of the cone, the owner and distributor of knowledge?

Perhaps, but we cannot really say. If knowledge opens differently, so do time and space. In such a new time-space-knowledge realm, is the self still active? What becomes of its role as knower? Is knowledge distinct from what manifests?

SIMULTANEOUS CREATION

When we looked earlier at the image of the cone of time as a model for the history of the universe, we found ourselves asking about the time 'before' the beginning of time: the other side of the temporal zero. The fullness of zero, its 'many-sidedness', reminded us that 'before' the beginning, time would not be bound by the cone. It might unfold in many directions—or even all directions—simultaneously.

Could the same be true for knowledge? If knowledge is no longer bound by the structure of the subjective cone, what would prevent it from taking any point in space or time as 'here'? Certainly the complete allowing of zero gives us permission to make this move. What would happen if we switched our usual 'here' with 'there'? What if we traded 'now' and 'then'?

For a 'global' knowledge, there would be no basis for affirming the lines that separate 'this' zero from 'that' zero. The distinctions that the cone unfolds and enforces would prove in a sense to be arbitrary, based on borders and barriers that have no substance. Although time proceeds, it is the same in each moment; although space offers multiplicity, it remains utterly open.

Can knowledge really operate with this kind of complete freedom? Let us make a simple thought experiment. Five billion years ago, the earth took form. Can knowledge reverse that vast accumulation of history? Clearly our subjective knowledge cannot. But even on the subjective level, we are able to look backward: to imagine time moving backward and to trace out the sequencing through which the present has come to be.

True, such a 'subjective' reversal does not affect the forward progression of time through the length of the cone. But how much weight should we assign to the stubborn solidity of the past as we have come to know it? If we reverse time in our minds, letting knowledge claim the zero, does time still unfold with the same dogged determination in external reality?

Perhaps we could rethink the relationship of knowledge to time. Can knowledge make the future into the past? Can it keep the 'from' but give up the 'to'? What happens if knowledge abandons the 'from/to' framework, with its specific sets of structuring tendencies, completely?

There may be other alternatives. For example, we usually assume that time and space remain as they are; that they are confined to their place in somewhat the same way that the ocean is confined to its bed by the force of gravity. Just as we cannot fall into the sky, we cannot fall 'away' from first-level space and time and the directionality and dimensionality they impose. But suppose we move to a second level. If we return to the zero, perhaps time and space can go everywhere and all at once, without regard for even a single one of the structures we take for granted. Perhaps they have already gone, or never arrived. If so, what holds knowledge back from joining them on their journey?

The structures that establish the frame for subjective knowledge are given by time and space. 'Here' is a space-time construct that makes possible 'there'. The baseline between them, as specified by time-space axes, gives the senses (including mind) something to work with, and on this basis directions and dimensions take form, opening from the zero-point. All this is well-known to us, even if the vocabulary and the way of thinking we are using to explore it here seem rather unusual. But why should this familiarity limit us? True, time and space can produce this much. But surely they can produce much more! If space has no edge, we can imagine a billion universes like this one, stacked on top of one another like pancakes. If time radiates from the zero-point in all directions, what has happened is not gone, and what is yet to come is everywhere available.

There seems no reason that knowledge cannot engage these possibilities. Looking back, we are right here; looking ahead, the potential is actual. The structures that we have been able to carve out of space and time are like waves on the ocean, or perhaps like a sandcastle on the beach. Whatever we have named is not it; whatever we have described is too restrictive. More is available, and more beyond that more, and still more. Must we really assign such vast importance to what is happening here and now? Must we really look for a source for experience elsewhere?

Zero of Knowledge

Is space appearance—space as zero—accessible to knowledge? If so, how does that accessibility function? If zero makes itself available to knowledge, what will be disclosed? And what must knowledge be like in order to conform to the zero of space?

The structure we have been exploring suggests that when zero is narrowed down to a point of view, knowledge constructs a baseline, and from the baseline a cone. Yet within the cone, at the center of the starting point, the fullness of 16, which is also the fullness of zero, remains available.

From a space-centered way of understanding these two levels, zero stands for the holding power with which space endows appearance: the power to manifest space and form, existence, appearance, phenomena, and reality. From a time perspective, zero is the energy of time that makes accommodation possible: the chance that gives the opportunity. Now let us look from a knowledge perspective. How does knowledge understand zero to operate?

ACCESS THROUGH THE AXES

I n the established world of matter and mass, gravity and linear temporality, zero plays the role of point of origin. In this capacity, as 'ground zero', it serves knowledge as meeting point for 'up' and 'down' and 'here' and 'there'. It makes possible locatedness in physical space.

Suppose there were a different space, a 'beneath' of physical, first-level space, akin to the 'prior' of time. Could zero serve knowledge differently? Could it be a transition to that space?

Do we have any evidence that such an 'inner' space is available? Appearance itself may be the best evidence. For space as it operates in the physical realm can never account for its own emerging, or for its own power to allow. Only a 'space' expansive enough to accommodate both space and all its contents seems capable of the holding power that gives being permission to come forth. If there are theories that attempt to account for how gravity, properties, and the distance-making of conventional space operate, we can at least count the 'beneath' of space as one such theory.

If the zero-point marked a point of transition to an inner, second-level space, that would not mean that inner space lies hidden at a specific spatial location (for instance, at the temporal point of origin). This view remains too closely bound to baseline, cone, and background. Instead, the inner accommodation that appears with zero is better understood as available everywhere, in all the 16 directions of fullness, like a balloon expanding in 16 dimensions at once.

The axes that accompany the zero-point could serve as a symbol of this possibility. In giving birth to the zero-point, the axes point back toward the womb of space. They invite knowledge to look *through* the specific modes of thinking and knowing in force within the domain of the cone. The axes give access.

We might think of each point that conventional knowledge specifies as always collapsing back into the access of the axes. This suggests an axiom: Each point is a singularity, akin to the 'black holes' of physical space. It 'incorporates' in its appearing the whole of space.

FOUNDING EXISTENCE

Two kinds of space would mean two kinds of knowledge, one linked to the cone of conventional appearance, the other somehow more fundamental. What does this more fundamental knowledge have to say to us? Can we learn anything specific about how it would function, and toward what end?

Suppose we stretched out the whole of the physical universe, so that every point became almost zero. For a fundamental knowledge, such a transformation would presumably be of little significance. Yet that is not our ordinary perspective. Somewhere in this near-infinite domain would be the cone that puts my particular self at the apex of the cone. The specific zero-point that makes this occupancy possible is where we focus.

The zero-point of the cone establishes a foundation for conventional knowledge. Knowing things to be as they are, knowledge turns the fullness of point-being (the zero of each point) into the particulars with which we are familiar. We could say that zero allows this to happen. But what makes it possible? How can zero establish existence? If we understand this transition, we might understand as well the transition from first-level to second-level knowledge.

One answer to this question would be to say that zero need not establish anything, because nothing exists. But this goes against common sense, which knows that things exist almost as firmly as it knows the 'I am here'.

A second approach is to say that the properties of what exists are actually established in being known by the subject. But even if we say this is so, it leaves our question open: How does subjective knowledge bring this about? How does it turn zero into 'something', and on whose authority? What, we might ask, is the 'from' of the 'from'?

As another alternative, we could say that existence is 'there' but not established, or that existence dwells 'within' the zero-point and remains essentially space. Yet this answer is also not satisfying. On the first level, there is existence, and then there is space. The two do not seem to operate at the same level. If we held other-wise, how could we account for existence or particular-ity at all?

Even if we try to explain that we are speaking of a second, more fundamental kind of space, the question remains. Somehow there must be a transition; some-how the link between open space and the particulars of the knowledge cone must be made in a satisfying way.

TRANSITION THROUGH ZERO

L ooking for the point of transition returns us to the zero-point, available not only at the point of origin, but as the origin of every point. If the zero-point is to function as transition point, it must be able to hold what appears, to hold the whole. What appears does appear, and in this sense it has been established, but the holding of the whole must be more fundamental than this. To hold the whole means to let the point—the full-ness of the space-zero—emerge as the whole, informing the whole. We could imagine appearance without this wholeness, but such appearance would be pointless. Perception would proceed without a frame, and the point could not be made. It would not be possible to frame questions or get answers.

To make the point, to hold the whole, is to make the case fully. Because this fullness embodies the form wholly, answers can emerge. Is it in such fullness, then, that the transition is made? Is this how the whole of a fundamental knowledge becomes the certainty of the first-level knowledge that establishes as real?

In Western philosophy it has sometimes been argued that what is truly real is the realm of form, from which ordinary reality somehow emanates. That notion invokes a second-level order, and in this sense may be related to the inquiry we are conducting here. But there is also a fundamental difference. The form that marks the transition from fundamental to conventional knowledge comes to completion when the point holds the whole. Knowing the whole that the zero-point upholds, knowledge knows the 'prior' of the beginning and the 'beneath' of what appears. It knows 'within' the first-level structures of the cone, and it is just this knowledge to which the cone gives expression.

To say that the point must hold is thus to evoke the certainty of right knowledge: knowledge open to the fullness of what appears. Once such knowledge has been activated, once it has made the transition through zero into conventional space, appearance in all its usual dimensions and structures takes on a different significance. The baseline become the unfolding of value, meaning, quality, and truth.

To describe this transition, we might say that appearance emerges as the ratio between a higher-level knowledge and the ordinary patterns we name and identify. The baseline verifies the point, and the point establishes the ratio. The indication in practice is that existence moves readily toward action and the meaningful. Not bound by repetition or not-knowing, it expresses a perfect clarity.

ZERO GROUND OF KNOWLEDGE

Right knowledge offers a potentially clarifying perspective on the zero-point and the structures it generates as an alternative to the ways of knowing with which we ordinarily operate. First-level knowledge depends on such 'operators' as measurement, size, direction, and distance. Together with the ratio, these factors allow for distinction and proportion, for names and other artifacts of language. But the structures of the zero-point, including points and cones and baselines, provide a different way of knowing, one that is not bound by first-level structures.

The zero-point can ground a way of knowing that proceeds with a kind of mathematical precision. Zero 'reads' space or expresses it, in such a way that higher-level knowledge remains available. Zero-based operations allow for an interpretation of the ratio that does not give existence the same weight or gravity. They allow knowledge to go ahead without presuppositions, so that appearance can express the fullness of knowledge.

Seen in this way, zero transforms the 'is' that is implicit in every element of the first-level 'I am here'. A first-level 'is' takes the manifestations of shape and form and makes them concrete. It assigns them the substance that we associate with objects and with reality. In this view, appearance has only one message to communicate, which is its own existence. Other possibilities are lost or forgotten.

With the zero-based mathematics of the point and the cone, however, knowledge can turn from the surface of appearance that the 'is' attempts to solidify. It can enter the depth of space, the 'beneath' of appearance, discovering the multidimensional dance of zero in space.

Before space had been preoccupied by the shapes and forms with which first-level knowledge concerns itself, the depth of space was already available. Zero holds open within each ratio this 'other' space, this depth that is also the 'prior' of the beginning.

Ordinary knowledge has no way to access this depth. For its existence-based mode of seeing, only those points can be observed that previous points of reference point out, and only those ratios are available that the senses are prepared to take into account.

Operating with such knowledge, we know size and shape and particles and perspectives, but we do not know space. We can talk about space only after it is filled up. For instance, the very idea that there might be a past of space or a future of space, is virtually meaningless. And since this is so, we have no way to understand the present depth of space.

Still, knowledge itself is not bound by these limits. That is why zero and the geometry it evokes seem able to play a vital transitional role, opening the fullness within appearance that reveals the depth of space. Perhaps we do not yet know how the transition is possible; perhaps it seems no more than theory. Yet simply to speculate that space could have a prior, that appearance could have a within, marks a major shift. Matters could play themselves out differently.

AVAILABILITY OF FULLNESS

From our ordinary perspective, the fullness of a higher knowledge might manifest first in a sense that something is missing, that we have lost touch with the time, space, and knowledge of our own being, and are operating on a level of incompleteness. Perhaps we have known times when such a feeling arose within us, a longing for something indefinable, or a feeling of time passing without meaning or significance.

A perspective grounded in knowledge itself would look on this feeling of loss and incompleteness with a kindly disinterest. But this does not make such feelings irrelevant. If the experience of incompleteness arises within the cone, it will offer its own axes of access, its own zero-points of fulfillment. In fact, the sense of longing and incompleteness may be an especially powerful point of access, one that we should not let pass by lightly or try to avoid.

Other, similar feelings may likewise give access to a different knowledge. For instance, the self thinks it owns time and acts in time, but the idea of ownership itself arises in time. As an aspect of the whole, it could give access to the whole, provided we approached it with that intention in mind. Feelings of being lost are another such point of access. Could we let ourselves feel lost, and at the same time cultivate the perspective that there is no such thing as being lost, that the whole always holds?

At a deeper level of knowledge, the various dichotomies of ordinary knowledge (such as have/have not, know/not know, right/wrong) would be changeable, transferable, even reversible. Could that become our perspective? If we try to put it into effect, what happens?

If we actually try to experiment with such perspectives, we should keep in mind the need to proceed at two levels at once. With greater knowledge, gain and loss become a matter of only minor concern, as if we had come into possession of a new and more valuable currency that we can use to replace the old. We could truly say that only in the realm of difference does difference make a difference. Yet at the same time, we do inhabit that realm. It seems important to acknowledge that the distinction between lower-level and higher-level knowledge is also not binding. At a third level, both could be seen as united. Each is acceptable, and there is no contradiction.

BODIES OF KNOWLEDGE

As an analogy for the interplay among the different levels of knowledge, consider again the Giant Body exercises introduced in Part I of *Time, Space, and Knowledge*. There the suggestion is made to investigate the body by going into it in the imagination, visualizing each component from the perspective of a tiny observer, and to gradually proceed to ever smaller physical domains. In this investigation, it is vitally important that the body being investigated is a living organism, its parts interacting with one another in a highly coordinated way.

Observing these interactions, the question arises: What makes the whole? What confirms the connections that space provides? Many answers could be given, but for our present purposes we could reply that the awareness of the observer plays this role, by letting us see the whole in operation. How can the observer function in this way? Only by integrating the whole of what appears in space and interacts in time: the whole that space holds. In leading toward the discovery of space as the fundamental of appearance, the Giant Body reminds us that space can play this role only if it is also the *knowledgeable* realm that *Time, Space, and Knowledge* calls "just interactions and shining outlines."

Freedom
of Sixteen

We have called the fullness of zero '16'. Why single out this aspect of zero? Because there is no way to operate directly on the zero-point, which is not there. Even if 16 can be understood from one perspective as a reflection of zero, it is through such reflections that appearance takes form.

In the ordinary way of knowing, it makes no sense for 16 to emerge from zero. Specific sets, such as sixteen, manifest only as the cone unfolds. As knowledge presents constructs or theories, different dimensions are specified and identified, taking form along certain lines. Thus, science unfolds in the context of empirical, measurable data; philosophy in the context of logical inquiry; psychology in the context of the human personality or fundamental human traits. Systems depend on their background.

16, however, operates at a more fundamental level. Any point as zero-point offers the whole of 16. There is no unfolding, no specifying, and no assigning of attributes. We can find the unity of the whole anywhere; we can make any point the center.

If 16 were a conventional structure or designation, it would establish a point that departed from zero. It would introduce substance, meaning that we would either have to accept it, go through it, or find our way to the other side. But space establishes no such point, and in 16, space remains at the center.

DYNAMICS OF 16

We can understand 16 as a symbol for the fullness of the whole. We might think of it as the magical body of space, active within the zero-point, or as the coming to finity of space-infinity, free from every edge or border. It is the sixteen-colored rainbow that emerges from the pure white light of knowledge, the making of all points and the capacity to go in all directions. It is the boundlessness of the whole.

As the fullness of zero, 16 could be considered the foundation for appearance, the floor that must be there before the telltale click of shoes can be heard. 16 allows for transition, like lifting the foot in order to move forward. A focus on transitions thus seems an especially effective way to understand what 16 is pointing toward.

In transition, something appears from an undifferentiated whole. 16 allows for such appearance, and thus for the ratio, the measurement that specifies the conditions for the cone and for each specific alternative the cone can entertain. Through 16, knowledge can know the ratio and transmit the transition.

16 could be considered the finest, most subtle differentiation and the fullest expression of zero. It is the ratio of space and time in concert that makes them available to knowledge. At each moment and in each point, through the transition from zero, the 'x' of the axis becomes 16. Comprehending this, knowledge gains access to the fullness of the axis, which operates 'before' and 'as' the basis for the cone.

For conventional knowledge, 16 operates most visibly as the foundation, the axiom that founds the order. When we say that the axiom is the indisputable, the foundation beyond questioning, we are speaking in terms of concepts, but we may actually be pointing to 16 as the 'pointness' of the point.

When the axiom of the axis measures out the ratio of conventional appearance, the transition can be supported, and time in the conventional sense can unfold. 16 becomes the giving point, the holding of the whole that allows the cone to take form. Given by 16, the whole never becomes solid. Because it remains open, its fullness remains accessible to knowledge.

Through such access, knowledge remains true to its own unfounded nature. As the ratio of appearance to zero, 16 is also the ratio of knowledge to space. Recast as zero, available to knowledge, 16 is the secret source of every number, all directions, and each distinction. It allows form and matter to emerge.

In the freedom of 16, even the axes can be reconceived. The 'x' that marks the meeting point can intersect in different ways; its angles can be rotated differently; its dimensions can expand. There is no danger of collapsing into the void of a zero that negates what appears.

16 supports appearance and its underlying order rather than undermining it; 16 preserves substance without solidifying it. Offering the ratio, 16 gives each point the foundation for boundless transition. Appearance can emerge without being claimed by a knower. Order can take form, and rhythm can manifest.

BRINGING INTO FOCUS

To bring into focus the connection between 16 and the possibilities for knowledge, we can start with the kind of focus found in first-level understanding. First-level knowledge aims at clarity: the carefully conceived concept, the clearly remembered image, the edge of the leaf, the cause of the effect, the logic of the argument. Clarity lets knowledge frame experience in meaningful ways, so that the ratio can function and the point can hold. When this does not happen, time, space, and knowledge, even in their ordinary aspects, fail to enter the fullness of being.

As suggested in the discussion of space above, we might think of this way of being, which is less than the whole, as never reaching the 16, as stopping short at '15', or even before. Without insisting on the particulars, we might say that with 15 all is ready for the move toward substance, but the decisive point has not yet materialized. This happens with 16, the cutting edge, which establishes the ratio and lets the point hold the whole.

This image helps clarify a possible confusion. If all appearance depends on 16, if 16 is universally available, why the need for special efforts to turn knowledge toward fullness? The answer comes: In our ordinary understanding we do not necessarily engage the whole of 16. With time and space reduced to the rigid structures of measurement and distance, knowledge does not readily open to the fullness of presence. We are subject to confusion; we lack clarity; we miss the decisive point. We can only piece together and juxtapose, constructing a facsimile of the point: a viewpoint that we make our own.

DEMOCRACY OF 16

I t may help clarify this distinction to see how it applies in a particular setting. Let us take as our example political structures. As members of a democratically structured society, we claim the right to hold our own views and further our own positions, to express our opinions and act on our convictions.

From a knowledge-centered perspective, however, a society organized on this basis may not be expressing the true nature of democracy at all. When individuals take positions without having first reached the decisive point in their own understanding, knowledge fails to cohere. Even if all citizens could come together to express their views, engage in discussion, vote their preferences, and frame policy. the outcome would only be a summing up of this incoherence. Bringing to the ratio everyone's views would still not reach the clarity that brings real knowledge. After all the speeches and debates, the advertisements and appeals, the point would not be made.

What would a more knowledge-centered democracy look like? Without attempting to specify institutions or structures, we can at least say that in such a democracy, all points of view would meet in such a way that they became one—that the cutting edge emerged. For the decisive point is the meeting point for every other point: the ratio of the whole. Attuned to the fullness of 16, knowledge gains access to the ratio that resolves into right action.

Living 'Out of Focus'

On the personal level, not to arrive at 16 means not performing at our best. We might think in terms of being at various stages of development: '7', '13', '15', and so on. Operating at these levels, we tend to give in to daydreams or sleepiness, or fall into darkness or vagueness. We find ourselves not remembering the where, when, and how of what is happening, or losing sight of the guiding vision. We experience various conflicts, or find that our consciousness is governed more by moods and emotions than by insight or intention.

Living in this way might be almost like being drugged: dense, cozy, shut down, with little sense of time passing. There might be repeating images, but no clear, fresh thoughts. We might have the feeling that something has been left undone or ignored, without being able to specify what it is. Living out of focus, could we be clear on what is happening or who we are?

There are also more subtle ways in which we fail to make the point and arrive at the whole. For instance, do we really know that we will die, or is this final ratio covered over with uncertainty or a willful ignorance? Do we ask ourselves how much of our time has already gone by, and whether we are making the best use of the time remaining? Do we let ourselves notice how many opportunities for knowledge we have let slip away?

When 16 becomes available, a feeling of clarity and conviction may manifest. Such feelings may come in moments of great anger or great compassion, or when our minds are suffused with a feeling of inner peace. Experience takes on a strong, clearly defined shape: We feel fully present in our bodies, alert to our senses, and alive to what is happening. We act with a sense of certainty that mirrors the fullness of being whole.

In cultivating higher-level knowledge, arriving at 16 is surely only an intermediate step. But unless we reach the decisive point, our efforts will remain out of focus and out of register. No matter what we tell ourselves, they will never amount to much. Like someone looking unwittingly at the light from a star long since dead, we may be looking for knowledge in experience that presents only a confused shadow of the whole that 16 offers.

ALLOWING TRANSITION

At 16, a specific something emerges through an act of transition. A border is built up and a system established. The momentum of this happening could be assigned to time, but the establishing itself takes place through knowledge. 16 as the decisive point becomes the knowledge-point—the point of transition.

If transition takes place, it does so without obstruction, through a mechanism that never fails. For to say that the transition might not happen is to say that time might stop in its tracks, or space divide into segments that do not allow each other access. This is not our world.

The mechanism for transition is the ratio. Through the ratio, space is not solid and time not dead, and knowledge retains the power to shape what appears. For the ratio brings the difference that allows transition. Everywhere and in every moment, the ratio represents a second-level openness, maintaining the freedom that is the promise of 16. The dynamic of its curve has no terminating edge and no excluding solidity.

WHOLENESS OF ZERO

As the decisive point, 16 is not an amorphous or invisible background to appearance, a universal 'everywhere'. Nor is it a flourish on the substance of appearance, something added at the end. Instead, it is a structure with its own precision and order. It reveals itself geometrically, opening into a space and time in which all points are connected, all 16s one. Presenting the point-being of appearance, the specific transitions of 16 invite an order rooted in fullness.

The three-dimensional zero we first discovered in our inquiry into space points toward the fullness that 16 embodies. But it may be that 16 ultimately depends on a more fulfilling fullness: not just the zero before our eyes, but a zero that pervades all appearance. At that point it may be that the fifteen 'prior' moments of 16 each become 16—that each depends on every other, that the links between them are also all 16, and that all such 16s join in a wholeness more fundamental than the three dimensions of conventional space and time.

Suppose that every given point of space, in every moment of time, has sixteen possibilities. Could we say that the ratio that manifests in form arises through the knowledgeable interplay of those possibilities: those that become actual and those that do not? Could we say that the point completes itself in every moment?

Knowledge
Taking Shape

S omething comes into being through a point of origin,
exploding into appearance out of nothingness. Conventionally we explain such a happening by looking for
a causal connection. A power has built up and now it
discharges: The point emerges as response or reaction.

All this takes place in accord with the limits that
the prevailing structure allows, and these limits are
reflected in the facticity of the point. That is the law of
the law, the equation that generates the shapes and
forms of experience. Only the ear can hear an echo, and
only the eye can see the reflections of light off water.
There seems to be a kind of chemistry at work here, a
structuring that allows only specific reactions. Just as
stars convert hydrogen into helium to generate light, so
presupposed elements and invisible structures interact
to give rise to the light of knowledge.

As 16 unfolds zero in space and time, it expresses
such underlying structures, each consistent with the

knowledge appropriate to that space-time. Different shapes take form, different properties assert occupancy. All takes place in accord with a certain range of possible shapes and happenings, including our own capacity for understanding.

We could think of ratios as the expression of such hidden structures. They are curves in space or time, relationships between what manifests and what does not, distinctions growing out of the dynamics and mechanics of appearance. Pursuing this thought, we could speak of a ratio of the whole, an interplay that engages a range of related phenomena. Something like this may be what early astronomers felt they had discovered: beautiful harmonies and proportions in the cosmos that demonstrated the existence of an intelligent ordering principle in the universe. The formulas and equations of the physical sciences and mathematics could be thought of as ratios in this sense as well: descriptions in numerical terms of interactions that reveal the underlying order in the appearances that time and space present.

The ratio reveals other underlying orders. For example, the ratio of first-level time to first-level space assures that objects will appear throughout past, present, and future, separated by physical space, moving smoothly from one moment to the next. Nothing gets stuck at a particular point, and no event refuses to budge from the moment that it occupies, or jumps arbitrarily to another moment. The uninterrupted flow of this momentum allows for certain kinds of differentiation, each of which has its own ratio. In this sense, the ratio measures the difference between what can be attributed or possessed and what cannot. It is the ratio of the included to the excluded, of 'does' to 'doesn't'.

If 16 expresses zero, we might speculate that the ratio gives form to the axes that locate the zero-point. From the perspective of the ratio, the axes offer stability. They transmit the gravity of the background, linking it to an emerging directionality that in turn supports dimensionality. For instance, we could imagine that the particular curve that the axes make assures that in the order in which we move, space will manifest matter and experience will arise in time.

In fulfilling this function, the axes become the axioms of the order, sustaining the ratio of the whole (linked to what elsewhere has been called the 'logos'). But if the ratio becomes directly accessible to knowledge, the axes might well become more fluid in their possibilities. Now they could preserve the potential for openness implicit in the zero. Joined with knowledge, they could allow for new axioms to emerge.

CURVE OF GRAVITY

The link between the axes and the ratio proceeds through the baseline. It was suggested above that the baseline will never be completely straight, for the 'I am here' gives one end of the baseline, and the presence of the 'I' engages countless transitions in each moment, subjecting the baseline to the pull of our precise gravity. The curve of the line (and the weightiness of the 'from') give the ratio of experience: a pull shaped by meaning and purpose into structures such as linear time. Again, we could say that the line is not straight simply because we are guests of space—because we appear. For the moment something is happening, a ratio has taken form. Can such a 'taking place' take place without the forming of a curve?

Just as the ratio reveals that the baseline cannot be completely straight, so it establishes that it cannot proceed to infinity. Extending from the 'I am here', the baseline arrives at the 'there'. With 'here' and 'there' the 'I' makes its mark. It defines the background that the ratio measures out. From one perspective, such defining limits have no substance, but from another, they create another baseline. The ratio unifies these two alternatives, bringing them into harmony.

Each ratio measures out in a unique way the fullness of 16; conversely, we could say that each of the sixteen 'moments' of the zero-point has its own ratio. From a third perspective, we could say that 16 is the ratio for zero, the 'have/not have' that conforms to gravity, transition, and number. If the ratio failed to operate in these three distinct ways—if the curve of the ratio ceased to mark out—would appearance collapse?

INNER CODE

How would the ratio engage the second and third levels of time-space-knowledge? At the second level, the ratio would open appearance to space and events to the dynamic of time. At the third level, it might become available as the intrinsic 'orderness' that supports the whole of what appears.

From the first level, such deeper levels may manifest in ways that remain indefinite and even obscure: an inner code of being, a sacred mystery, a secret structure. Having glimpsed such unknown structures, we try to pursue their manifestations, but first-level time cannot accord with their dynamic, and we easily misunderstand what we have seen. Indeed, the very sense of mystery, of the secret that manifests as sacred, could be seen as an expression of the inability of first-level time (and space) to reveal the ratio directly.

If knowledge is to break through these barriers to understanding, it seems important to investigate at the level of fundamental mechanics: point and axis, baseline, ratio, zero, and 16. For instance, if knowledge can get clear on the nature of the point as both inclusive and exclusive, the link between zero and 16 may become more clear. One response would be to abandon points, with their attendant distinctions, entirely. Another would be to acknowledge that the ratio can make its own point.

If the ratio became available to knowledge, could fixed positions in space and time no longer hold? When we know the ratio of a problem, there is no longer any problem—only the ratio. At this point, the mechanics of the ratio prove deeply significant for our relation to our world. The shifting ratio affects how we establish perceptions and consciousness and how we make distinctions, including the distinction between self and others.

Transforming the Ratio

T he ratio at present supports our perspective, but if we understand the ratio well enough to change it, we could likely change the current cycles of transition and sameness as well. Understanding the dynamic that the ratio sets in place would be like breaking a code—the message would be clear, and we could pass on a new message.

All this would happen readily, for knowledge of the ratio would already have initiated the transformation dynamic. In this sense, the ratio would reveal the ratio of light to darkness, or of deeper knowledge to the first-level knowledge that interacts with first-level space and time.

One characteristic of the first level seems to be that we do not understand knowledge as intrinsic to the system. That being so, we cannot fully cognize the system itself as a space-time-knowledge ratio. Caught up in personal reflection, concerned with 'my' position in the whole, we cannot engage time-space-knowledge as the threefold axes of the three-dimensional zero, the points of access of a third-level knowledge.

However, when higher levels of time and space open, knowledge increases accordingly. We could describe this by saying that the ratio of time to space to knowledge approaches unity, which is also the ratio of zero to 16. Space, time, and knowledge come together without possibility of separation. In such circumstances, would there be any distinction between knowing and not knowing? Any need to learn?

RATIOS OF PREDICTION

One way to develop knowledge is to study trends that reflect past, present, and future ratios. For instance, the transformation in our beliefs and convictions through history have allowed us to make unparalleled progress in some areas, but have certainly led to loss in others. Can we identify what is positive and what is negative in our present circumstances? How would we make the judgment in terms of social relations, forms of consciousness, or values; in our attitudes toward desire; in the ways that our knowledge has grown or decreased; in our understanding of how space and time operate and manifest in our lives? Could we work out the interactions in all these domains? Could we determine the series of ratios that gave to our present time its specific attributes?

What about the future? Can we say what will happen in the next twenty years or the next century? Can we say what lifestyles will come to the foreground, or where science or religion is headed? Will we follow our secular way of life to its logical conclusions? What role will there be for spirituality, for religion? What will happen with business, with government, with all the branches of education? What course will technology take? Which countries will become powerful, politically, economically, and militarily? Will power be decentralized or centralized, or both at once? What presently unimagined trends will emerge, and where will they take us? The answers to such questions may seem beyond our reach, but there are ratios available now that could suggest some directions.

We could look in the same way at patterns of the ordinary mind: at emotions and assumptions, at the trends toward anarchy and disorder on the one hand and totalitarianism and control on the other. Will individualism be the guiding force in coming decades? Where is the human psyche headed? Can we say which social and cultural trends are more powerful, and how they will play out in different regions of the world? Can we measure where our knowledge is headed? Will knowledge hold more power, or will it be money, or fame or influence? How will that power be used?

When secular approaches to life are in the ascendancy, the meaning of being alive tends to be viewed in terms of what each individual possesses; in other words, to specific ratios in the weakest and most limited sense. Can we estimate the ratio of that ratio? If it intensifies, will we lose the ability to question fundamentals? If so, what will become of the ratio of knowledge to the unknown?

Present knowledge seems unable to make reliable predictions regarding such matters. We lack all basis for quantification. Yet there may be other ways for knowledge to move toward certainty. In theory, might it not be possible to specify an entire particular existence, in all its details, in numerical terms? Just as DNA can be specified as a binary code, could every conceivable attribute be identified: its origin and end, its development and sequence, its properties and interactions?

Suppose we could truly do this. Surely there would be great value from developing such knowledge. Yet in the end, we would still be missing the whole of 16.

What is needed is a model for knowledge comprehensive enough to arrive at the ratio of this whole: at the 'what is now' and the 'what is still to come', the 'what will be' and the 'what once was'. Such a knowledge, not exhausted by the endless accumulation of specifics, might be able to specify differently. Perhaps it could operate through a different kind of mathematics not so closely linked to number, akin in some ways to the kind of inquiry we have been pursuing here.

If the elements exist, if they are there, what prevents their being specified? Pursuing this question, would we close in on a knowledge that spanned the three divisions of time and the dimensions of space? Perhaps if we could engage such a ratio, we could activate a knowledge that divided and specified in accord with specific attributes, arriving at the kind of first-level knowledge that now seems beyond our reach.

Even then, our specification might not be verbal. Perhaps it would manifest in gesture, or in sensation or action. Just at the point where we have no way to put into words, our knowledge might encompass 'here' and 'there', past and present and future—the entire dynamic of the whole.

This broader view of specification suggests that the power to specify is also the power to transform. Does something exist? Does it not exist? All this may be reversible. Shapes change, forms change. If appearance is given by zero, why should the specification of appearance through the ratio restrict the more fundamental shaping power?

Mathematics of Transition

D oes the dynamic of 16 engage the temporal rhythm that moves in a zig-zag pattern? When our senses have not been trained in the sensitivity that would disclose such patterns, it seems difficult to say. First-level time and space, unfolding through their own dynamic, establish obstacles to the knowledge that could determine such specificity. Knowledge cannot catch up with the way that time runs and cannot read out its manifestations. It is like trying to make sense of a text written in a different script that one can barely puzzle out: All the words turn into letters, and the meaning dissolves again and again.

If knowledge as presently constituted displays such shortcomings, it may be because it is too tightly bound to the past. Having forgotten the order implicit in appearance, we cannot forget, for even a moment, the order that we impose. Intent on shaping a world we view as recalcitrant material for our shapings, we affirm what has been established. Clinging to what has been determined, we cannot welcome what has yet to be. Unable to let go of the previous space, we cannot cognize the next one.

The ratio that determines such clinging insists on the past as origin. In each moment the past moves on, and a transition presents itself. But we do not let go, and so we cannot go along. Using ratio to support our subjective ways of knowing, we designate degrees of change, assigning priority to sameness. Unable to pronounce past, present, and future as simultaneous, we cannot enter the point-being or arrive at the 16. Unable to understand zero, we cling to the axes and wait for the feedback from the already projected. Our transitions take us only away, leave us only outside.

Suppose that somewhere, in this display of sameness, a secret code revealed the interconnections of 16. For us, it would be indecipherable. The ratios our knowledge allows reveal a world reduced to flatness. Like a mirror, our awareness reflects only one surface. Even if that surface resolves into points, and the points into prisms that display 16, we cannot hold the whole. If appearance appears, it is only as image or reflection.

How can knowledge read appearance at a deeper level? Perhaps it could rely on the inner structure of a different mathematics, which yields a different geometry and a different architecture. Starting at the zero-point, tracing out ratios, sensitive to the holding of the whole, a new recognition leads to its own transitions. New ratios give knowledge greater scope, suggest new images and metaphors, engage a newly available dynamic. In one sense, we are asked to let go of much of what we consider ours. But if we can make sense of this possibility, our 'making sense' becomes the gateway to transforming time and space. Knowledge then follows readily.

ALTERNATIVE GEOMETRIES

Imagine that the ratio opens—that new knowledge comes to the fore. Does this mean that space has expanded from a previous contraction? This may be our perception, but it seems more accurate to say that the opening of the ratio has nothing to do with expansion or contraction, or that it allows both without interference or contradiction. The ratio is not bound to one place; when it opens, we discover the points of space, the rhythms of time, and the distinctions of 'from' without regard to the 'here' and 'there' specified by first-level knowledge. We enter the meaningful geometry that discloses space, time, and knowledge directly.

At this point, the transitions of experience can be differently observed. Rather than remembering or forgetting the past, we can inhabit it. Inhabiting it, we can let go of it. Letting go of it, we are able to specify the future, not at a distance, but from within. The tenseness of our present way of being can give way.

We think of time as a river, or a cone whose axis stretches out through time. But suppose that time were a sphere. Would the structures that knowledge specifies in this moment hold for all time? Perhaps it would all look completely different, like taking a cross-section of the cone and discovering . . . flatness? . . . zero?

Moving from cone to sphere, whether in time or space, is not a matter of traversing or even opening more space in the conventional sense. Though the universe is expanding, it is infinity that holds the power of the ratio. Where this power is engaged, territory is without significance. Momentum and transition do not go outside of space, nor do they move. Dimensionality does not differ, but is still transformed. As an analogy, consider: What is the ratio of a black hole to its surrounding space?

The decisive shift comes with the realization that the cone itself, together with the ratios that frame it and the points that define it, is open space and that shape is only another part of the ratio. Then the sphere can become the ground for the cone. The two are interpenetrating, even coextensive. We can see both at once, without contradiction. We can determine their time-space-knowledge ratio.

Transition to Knowingness

Suppose that space and time make up all that is: that space allows appearance and time conducts the aliveness of experience. What is the role of knowledge? Looking to each emerging ratio, each determined distinction for an answer, we see a trinity of interpenetrating dualities—space taking form through time and knowledge, knowledge through time and space, time through space and knowledge—interactions we could imagine in the form of a six-pointed star. Clearly time, space, and knowledge do not establish separate domains. They must meet somewhere, even if it is not in the three dimensions with which we are familiar.

Reframing the Ratio

Imagine that time, space, and knowledge were all available fully. We might imagine this to be the ratio of 1:1:1, but would it be a ratio at all? Ratio measures distinction and degree; for instance, the ratio of shadow and light, brightness and dullness, clarity and confusion. If all is optimal in the working of the time-space-knowledge trinity, is there any need for ratio?

Suppose that in the whole of 16, the light of knowledge opens, and its shining (which we call awareness) enters time and space. When this light is at its purest, does gravity function? Does rhythm enact? Or does the ratio merge into zero?

At 15, the baseline is in place, but in the 16th moment comes transition: the cutting edge, the possibility of coming to be and the possibility of not being possible alike. Suppose that the ratio owes its origin to the lightness of this freedom, this ability to be 'toward' anything at all. Would the power of the ratio to determine somehow be cut? Or would this possibility allow for thoughts that were not so heavy, for accepting the distinctions of language without enthroning its namings? If we learned to follow such freedom into opening, could we say that knowledge was learning itself?

It is natural for us to place knowledge at the apex of the time-space-knowledge triangle, mimicking the cone of knowledge. But suppose that knowledge were instead a host of sixteen armies of liberation, moving up the sides of the cone, restoring zero to zero. If knowledge emerged victorious, would consciousness change? Would the frame of knowledge stand revealed? Would positions disclose the act of positioning?

In first-level knowledge, we make use of a frame for our ideas and identifications: the background of the axes. But if the ratio of knowledge shifts toward the fullness of 16, our way of thinking and identifying may change as well. The need for the limiting frame may diminish. As the ratio moves toward wholeness and the zero-point opens, the cone is transfigured. Does the usual frame still function?

The frame is subjective. Grounded in the background, it affirms 'I am here' and the beginning, the 'from', and the opposition to the object. But if 16 can emerge fully, the quality of mind may change. No longer bound to a specific ratio, the situation becomes more fluid. The need to hold on to positions may fall away.

With such a loosening, it seems natural to move toward a knowledge of knowledge. We are in a position to see how psychology and science and other systems of knowledge are set up. We can see how, as ordinary human beings, we likewise set up beliefs and thoughts and the structures of mind, making interconnections that depend on taking up our accustomed positions.

In such an inquiry, we may discover that we have been followers, trained in habits that strip us of the freedom to be otherwise. We may recognize that we have been living under a secret tyranny: the human consciousness regime, the governing system that dictates to us all truth and values, and stimulates in us the responses (guilt and fear, desire and pride, self-image and identity) that maintain the regime in power.

The turning point comes when knowledge expands to include the 'I' as knower, the 'I am here' at work fabricating the framework. Now we can look at ratios as neither true nor false: We can look wholly without judgment. In each moment, the 16 is available. 'Right' and 'mistaken' no longer exert the same hold on our awareness. In fact, if we look with the right eyes, what is wrong may be very inviting, opening to a far more pervasive knowledge than we had been exercising under the old regime.

If we want to be exempt from patterns and positions, this kind of inner penetration is deeply valuable. The ongoing crisis can be our thesis, the starting point for knowledge to unfold. We can recycle the garbage, seeing any circumstance as an expression of the knowing activity.

If the 'I' is the one that knows, none of this will be possible. But if knowledge is open to 16, and if the 16 points of 16 all express knowledge through their own 16, the only owner of knowledge is knowledge. The more we come alive to this prospect, the more spontaneously we pass on knowledge to others so that each transition is a new transmission. 16 becomes a kind of sacred duty, but one that imposes no burden. Our load could not be lighter, and each step on the journey brings new joys.

When every point is the zero-point, every point holds knowledge. Fullness opens, without substance that could give separation. 16 yields ratios, and ratios give shape, distinctions, measures, and distance, all of which in turn are labeled as new variants in different languages and different disciplines. Even as distinctions sharpen, the underlying knowingness remains available everywhere.

TURNING TOWARD COMPLETENESS

How can we assess our present knowledge in light of the possibilities for a knowledge of the whole? For instance, is this culture truly in the vanguard of world history? Do we know how to evaluate the quality of the life we are living? How to make comparisons? If we have been performing tasks that have no meaning, does that make our life meaningless? If we have destroyed much that has value, have we become the instruments of hate? Looking at the special qualities of this time, we can value the information we have accumulated and the vast power we wield. But what is our own position? What do we have to offer? Can we profit or benefit from knowledge? Can we live in a better way than before?

Certainly our circumstances are not perfect; surely they could be improved. But how are we to begin? Are there ways to implement knowledge, to conduct differently? Are there different models to put into effect?

A good starting point is to understand what we human beings have been doing until now. Knowing the past, we can see conditions and recognize consequences. We can acknowledge who we are and see the future likely to result if we continue in the same way. Recognizing this, knowing that the patterns we follow are followed by others as well, we can see how events and patterns join together to form an unbroken chain. Seeing how each supports and depends on the other, we can see as well how the outcome takes on the quality of fixed and absolute certainty.

In today's society, the knowledge at work has certain clear consequences: an accelerating pace of change, a lack of true innovation, a sense of being at the mercy of unknown factors that lead to unforeseen difficulties. A powerful impulse to claim everything as 'mine' fosters a breakdown of communication. Cycles of limitation and scarcity proliferate, not so much on the level of material wants as in the sense of meaning and fulfillment that makes a life worth living.

This picture is dark. Does it apply with special force in our own time? Or do similar patterns emerge whenever the transitions that power the cycles of human life are grounded in incomplete knowledge?

Why should we accept limitation at all? Time, space, and knowledge, the very substance of our being, are always available. If we let ourselves enter the network of their interaction, we move naturally to the fullness of 16, where everything is possible. We do not have to be the bystander or bias-stander, the outsider and commentator. We can be in it completely. We can give it our best shot.

KNOWLEDGE THE ORIGINATOR

Within ordinary time and space, the patterns that have already been established propagate themselves forward. Like a rock rolling downhill, everything moves along lines of least resistance to the lowest point. The point is lost, its being is dissipated.

Yet sometimes a special curvature reverses this trend. As forces pull on us in all directions, we arrive at a point of perfect balance, a point of singularity. The coin we toss in the air lands on its edge and stays there. The moment does not end. Harmony prevails.

The prospect for such singularity comes from knowledge. In knowledge, each point is newly born, like a camera shutter clicking open. Time and space are available in the fullness of 16, poised before locatedness and within happening. The ratio has not yet been formulated. The transition endures.

At this point of being newly born, 16 has not yet sponsored the ratio. Positive and negative, possible and impossible, being and not-being are all in perfect balance. The decisive and determining point is yet to come. In a sense, we are beyond 16.

We might say it is not knowledge that originates or sponsors such a balance, but rather the being of the point. Yet these two views merge. To become being, the point enlists the support of time and space, and thus *arrives* at knowledge. Now the ratio can move forward; now it is possible to proceed. For in the end, knowledge determines how time shall act and space shall be.

Through knowledge, we see, pursue, and know; through knowledge, we convert, transform, and understand. If time and space give all possibilities, knowledge gives choice.

This point of choice is the balance point. It is the wholeness of the circle, radiant with rays of light, emerging in the time-space-knowledge trinity. Just this circle is the point of origin for the baseline: the zero-point source for the cone. And so we can say, joyfully: Knowledge remains available.

TRANSITION TO KNOWLEDGE

The usual terms we use for knowledge are linear in their connections and implications. We speak of a point of origin and a zero-point, but in fact every point is zero and every zero moves toward transition. Each transition is also a point, also an axis, also an axiom. Each axis is a ratio, and each ratio is 16. Each ratio allows for expansion and contraction, the archetypes of the rhythms of unfolding and establishing through which appearance manifests.

How can this be expressed in a way that makes sense? How can we engage time and space and knowledge in a dialogue that proceeds at all levels and maintains all possibilities?

Let us look more closely at the notion of transition. Transition is what makes it possible to go from here to there. But transition requires elements that transit: building blocks or units for transition. Certain shapes and forms occur, based on the ratios of the previous. Measures are established through many small differences. Emerging out of a background, the 'from/to' transition takes form, suggesting purpose that can inform the ratio.

DECISIVE POINT

The fundamental transition remains available within the determined ratio, but only in a way that is mysterious, almost magical. The ratio specifies that there has been change and allows as well for future change. It determines a first condition and then a difference; for instance, a curve in space that takes on different forms through time.

But how is it that change comes? What accounts for the transition? Why did the original condition not continue? At what point did the change occur? And what is the degree of change? The ratio specifies all this as well, giving the ratio of difference and the ratio of degree. Through such specification, transition—founded on the ratio of 'was' to 'is'—becomes possible.

Can we say more? Can we make the transition from specification to a higher-level knowledge? The rhythms of words do not allow it, but the rhythms of knowledge may be more flexible. In the cone of subjective knowledge, the points are there, the gateways are there, the axes are there. The depth of 16 manifests, and transition becomes available. The decision is made: yes or no!

TRANSITION TO ZERO

First comes the axiom or the 'x', and then the baseline. But even before this, for every existent, is the point. Before the point, within the point, is zero.

Space has no properties, but it gives place, so that something can take place. Zero plays this role: the place-holder, occupying without occupancy, allowing without proclaiming. It allows the transition and allows taking form. Its 'no property' is not blankness; rather, it engages the 'not yet having taken place' of the transition.

Zero is knowable by nature. If we try to replace zero's 'no something' with a 'nothing', or even an 'unknown', knowability withdraws. Now we are making it all up: just talk! Strange that people have given their lives to defend the outcome of such talk.

What can transition make of zero? Conventionally, zero means non-existence and non-operation. It is the place-holder that does not do, the non-occupancy that has no properties and does not establish. With zero, the baby is never born; the background is not determined—not by 'by', not from 'from', and also not directly. We can speak of the uncreated or non-existence, but perhaps it is best to say nothing at all, for there is little to be said about what does not engage the human realm of what has been established.

Zero is also the point-being, holding the whole. It is 16, the manifestation of all transitions. At the zero-point, the 16 meet, and this meeting itself is a transition, grounded in the ratio of zero to 16 that gives the zero-point.

'Within' zero, 16 is there: space and time before matter, energy, and equations, open and simultaneous. With 16, the baby is born after all. 16 traces its curve through space-time-knowledge, displaying the transitions of shape and form.

In all the 16 directions zero founds every property as ratios of 16, degrees of 16, dimensions of 16: in 16 spaces, 16 points, each with its own 16. Only because these transitions continue can time unfold without break or interruption and space present without gaps. In each transition, the whole is present: the meaning of time itself, making transition possible.

If 16 is always active, can we speak of its absence or its withdrawal, or of its failure to mature? Perhaps we can say that when knowledge does not engage the wholeness of the whole, 16 falls asleep. Yet it is not necessarily our knowing or acting that makes the difference. How can we decide, when the knowledge we have available, and the space and time in which we carry out our measurement, do not fit the task? But if we do not decide, what is the determining unit? Is an answer necessary? Then let us specify the *th* of the thousand*th* or the million*th*: not separate, but also not ours to own.

Fourth Dimension

R atio gives interaction in the three dimensions: the interplay of time and space and knowledge, the link between past, present, and future; even the proportion of possible to impossible, 'happen' to 'not happen', and existence to non-existence. It seems to cover everything, everywhere. Then what is the origin of ratio? How does it arrive?

We have asked this question before, but let us look again, asking afresh. We can start with the transition through which a new ratio emerges. Any transition and any specification will do: It could be confusion, or a thought, or a visual image; it could be an elephant or the gross national product. If we ask after the giving point for this ratio—not in the abstract, but in that very case—we come to 16. But what gives content to 16? What is the being of the point-being?

When the ratio takes form, there is a phase transition. Until the very last moment, the final nanosecond, there is no telling what will happen, no way to distinguish impossible from probable from certain. Then how does that moment arise; how is the decisive point arrived at? Is it something that happens only rarely, as a singularity? We have identified such singularities, but only as a model for what is always available. For the decisive point is not only now and then; it is always emerging.

Here is a possible answer. If being emerges into the three dimensions of space and the three divisions of time, let us posit as its source a fourth dimension, where zero meets zero, where time, space, and knowledge connect. Let us imagine this dimension as the giving place for the ratio of 16.

A line on a plane is straight; the same line inscribed on a sphere follows the curve of the sphere. By extension, we could imagine that a line in a higher fourth dimension—one that encompassed the interplay of time and space and knowledge—would curve back on itself.

In this curve, would it produce the ratio of its own apparent being? Would it expand into the 16 of zero?

Perhaps knowledge would say all this very differently. Let us call the ratio as we know it the opening to a fourth-dimensional giving: the sign of the source. Could we say that each ratio goes to the edge of space: not as a limit, but as an opening? Would this going also be an act of creation? Would it be a being-point, with no source other than itself?

ESTABLISHED POINT

Once the ratio establishes a point, how does the next point arise? Is the transition abrupt or smooth? Does something jump from one moment to the next? Does one project into the other, or both into both? Has it all been set up in advance? The fourth dimension is the holding open of all these possibilities. It suggests movement in all directions simultaneously: the three dimensions of the three dimensions and the past-present-future of past, present, and future. Without disruption, without collision, it offers an inner directionality that links appearance and experience in time and space.

Does knowledge know this different mode of being to be so? Can it account for transmitting, or direct what exhibits? Perhaps yes, perhaps no. It is not a question for our knowledge, just as the fourth dimension is not the goal of our journey.

We might put it this way. If 16 is available everywhere and each moment brings a new ratio, does 16 move? How could it? Within the three dimensions of space and the threefold structure of time, where is there to go? Yet the ratio is always in transition. From where? To where? Not relying on 'source from', not proclaiming a secret origin or invoking an unknown, we invite the fourth dimension. Is there movement? Is there even reconfiguration of a constantly shifting whole? Is there finity as an expression of the infinite? Or does possibility emerge at a level that is more fundamental than these distinctions? Does possibility encompass even the impossible?

Four and Sixteen

Knowledge can inspire time and space toward the fourth dimension. Even if the meaning of this move escapes us, we may have no other chance.

Imagine that at the 16 of knowledge, we find a different time and space, a point of curving closure without limits, where knowledge merges with all possible expressions of time and space. Imagine that at each 16, the door to the fourth dimension stands open. Can we enter? It seems so simple, for 16 is always available.

The knowledge for our time-being does not know how. We hit the point and we bounce off; we zig and zag but cannot enter. The qualities that would grant entrance are not our qualities. The available is another: not distant, but unacceptable.

That is the challenge. How do we turn it all around, turn it inside out? How do we unframe the frame? What is the project for our current projection?

Perhaps it is not so difficult. However we choose to frame our prospects, our lives are a precious juncture of time, space and knowledge. Because 'I am here', the vast fortune of knowledge is available.

KNOWLEDGE OF BEING

The more we engage knowledge, the more we are returned to ourselves, to our own being. When we speak of space, we are speaking of our own bodies and minds. When we speak of time, we are reading out the qualities and characteristics of experience. When we speak of knowledge, we are looking toward territories and understandings that we ourselves have established. Time, space, and knowledge are the *here* of our being.

How can we approach the being of our being here? It will help if we are not too clever, not too quick to interpret. The moment we 'figure things out', we have lost the power of knowledge. Once we make it all 'make sense', space disappears, and we lose the meaning available 'between' the meanings we assign.

First-level knowledge makes surface connections, but knowledge that knows space and time directly knows the depth of here. It engages space and time, just as time engages space and knowledge and space engages knowledge and time. To engage means to embody, to embody means to live fully, and to live fully means to exercise time, space, and knowledge, so that they come into the fullness of being.

Knowledge that relies on making connections has its own standards for determining what is so. Drawing lines between this and that, linking and separating, it offers proof and probabilities, but it does not enter the depth of appearance. It never hits the target; it is always 'off'. If being is a full circle, 360 degrees, then such first-level knowledge can only be right 'to some degree'. It will never encompass the whole.

The gap between first-level knowledge and being is implicit in the mechanism of the ratio. Ratios distinguish and mark out differences; understood as the proper subject matter of knowledge, they do not arrive at presence, at being fully here. Relying on the outcome of ratios, first-level knowledge can make meanings clear: the right words emerge, and sense impressions confirm what has been presupposed. But even when such coordination creates a sense of knowledge in action, something is missing. From this first-level perspective, ratios stay on the surface. They make it possible to build connections in the form of reasons and explanations and distinctions, but they give no access to depth.

In such a way of knowing, the structure of the knowing act itself is 'off'. 'Pointing out' is off, and assigning identity is off. Looking for words or images or concepts is off, and so is looking for the field of the presentation or for 'I understand'. All these ways of knowing both miss the point and dismiss the depth of being.

They have already established a distance from space; they are already miles down the road. Time has passed them by, but they do not even notice. It is just this not-noticing that lets us imagine that the person who knows now is the same as the one who set out to know.

Once the point is missed, even if just by a few degrees, we have lost the chance to exercise knowledge by exercising time and space. We are cut off from direct engagement. We say the right words and have the right thoughts, repeating the patterns into which we have structured the presentations of time and space, but we find ourselves 'outside' instead of 'inside'. Even if we knock on the right door, even if we gain entrance, the party goes on without us.

For instance, when the subject sees an object, what does it really see? First-level knowledge, taking up its ratios, sees presence as the outcome of what has gone before. But from the depth of being, that view is 'off'. Presence does not emerge from a background—'here' does not arrive from somewhere else. Yet that is exactly how first-level knowledge understands things to be. The result is that you and I talk, but do not meet—we are not present to one another at all. The meaning is lost, and the point is missed.

If we are time, space, and knowledge, can we exercise this way of being? One test is in the relationship of knower to known. Could we cultivate a knowing without a ratio between subject and object? If the conventional 'between' does not operate at all, how does knowledge engage its object? Can we see?

233

Knowledge exercises being in questioning the structures of appearance. In the very middle of what is happening, can we ask about the who and the how? Can we see the mechanisms in operation? How do appearances manifest? What are the connections? What are the distinctions? How does first-level knowledge sort all this out, and what are the immediate consequences?

When we activate time, space, and knowledge within what is happening, it does not matter that we have missed the point or that we are still missing the point. Our missing the point is the point—the 'here' where being offers itself. Engaging the structures of first-level knowledge is our way of inviting knowledge into fullness. We are our own laboratory, our own ongoing investigation. Exercising being, we are not outside after all; we are in! The being we exercise is our own. The echo is only an echo, but the echo is also sound.

In this way of knowing, what becomes of the ratio? Ratios are indispensable to our way of being and knowing, and it would make little sense to discard them. True, ratios do not hit their mark. The next transition is already underway, and it is always too late to be certain. But the question is this: Can ratio merge with no ratio? Suppose that everything is a matter of degree: Can this first-level way of knowing merge with wholeness—with no possibility of misunderstanding and nothing left over?

We are accustomed to a style of knowing that takes one position and not the other, but for knowledge of being, positioning operates differently. We may be the ones applying for a loan from the Bank of Time Space

Knowledge, but we are also the banker. We may be actors in the story that time-space-knowledge tell, but we are also the storyteller, and time, space, and knowledge are our audience. Knowledge is ready to invite us in, so we are ready to enter.

THREE KEYS

The discovery that all points can be seen as symbols of zero could be considered the first key to opening the treasure-house of knowledge. Zero presents space in the shape of a point. Its defining edge marks the transition from the inner depth of point-being to the outer manifestations of appearance. Pointing out the depth of time and space, the zero-point introduces the fullness of meaning that time and space and knowledge can hold. It restores to knowledge the capacity to distribute such meaning throughout the space-time-knowledge realm of appearance.

From this foundation, knowledge can discover the second key: direct experience of the depth of being. Embodying space, uniting with space, knowledge experiences space-embodiment as warm and calming, free and open—like being balanced at the point of perfect equilibrium. Dwelling in the balance point, knowledge discovers the place for being fully alive.

The more space opens, the more readily knowledge can know the transforming wonder of engaging experience in time. Mind and senses and awareness unite with the fullness of presence, and all of time—past and present and future—become available. The provisional immediacy of here and now is transformed into a realm of aesthetic beauty and splendor.

At home in this depth of being, knowledge comes to realize that interpretations do not depart from direct knowledge, but rather express its power. Thought as thought is free to involve itself intimately with the senses and perception. What psychology examines as consciousness, what philosophy interprets as mind or awareness, what poetry understands as giving voice, art as inspiration, and religion as the divine that speaks within—all this becomes available within experience and form, as experience and form.

Integration at this level is the third key. Sheer wonder at all the ways experience can embody deepens into the final wonderment that knowledge can unite the depth of being and the expanse of appearance. United and available, moving to the same rhythm, time and space and knowledge contribute to the whole. An infinity of being opens—beyond concepts, thought, projections, or imagination, yet not cut off from them. Expanding with a momentum all its own, opening widely in time and space, knowledge embodies the Body of Knowledge. Inseparable from all potential throughout space and time, knowledge translates time into the being of here and now, fully engaging the being of the point. The 'I am here' enters the depth of fullness.

No saying can capture the whole of this transformation, which opens into the third level of time-space-knowledge. But it is possible to contemplate its benefits. The Body of Knowledge can extend throughout space the capacity of time to present experience. As this embodiment becomes our embodiment, we learn how to control time and how to retrieve from space unlimited bounty. We bring to each activity our own most profound capacities and discover within the treasures that we have always sought.

Beyond what can be put into words, without ownership, universally available, joy, love, and beauty radiate throughout time and space. We do not have to go somewhere else to find them, for the secret dimension of the sacred is here. Inquiry and inspiration lead us down the path, and wonderment unlocks the door. We enter a field of boundless fascination, of measureless creativity. We breathe the air of freedom, and know in our hearts the delight of awakening to full embodiment.

It is all past imagining. In the fullness of being, Great Knowledge provides Great Love. We can know our own knowledge, live our own time, open our own space. For everything is within space, and nothing that appears is separate from the mind that knows. In every moment, every point of thought can open, and every point of being can manifest.

What could be more wonderful? A life fresh and fulfilling; a new journey always underway. An adventure unfolds—in all dimensions, every moment . . . for every human being.

Illustrations

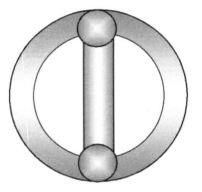

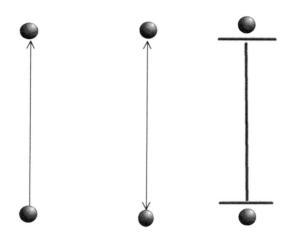

Here and There, Now and Then,
Subject and Object form a baseline.

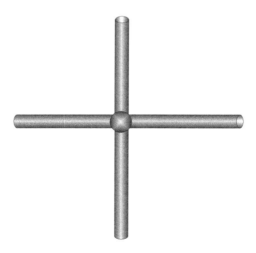

Two lines are required to locate a point,
an x-axis and a y-axis.

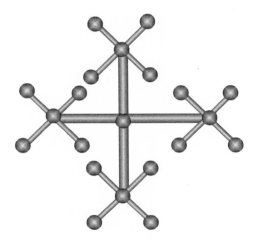

Each of the four endpoints requires two more axes to locate, giving a total of 16 points.

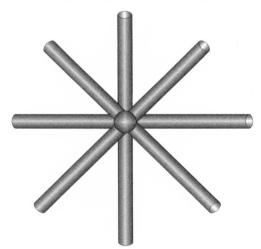

Rotating the two axes forty-five degrees gives an eightfold compass around a point.

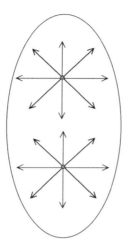

The eight lines of direction can also be doubled
and stacked together.

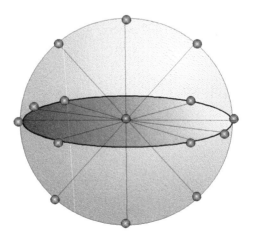

If one set of eight lines is rotated ninety degrees in the
third dimension, a sphere becomes apparent.

243

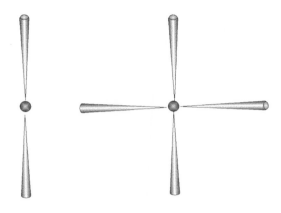

Along each line of direction, a cone can begin to develop from each side of the zero-point.

Cones develop in all directions
from all sides of the zero-point.

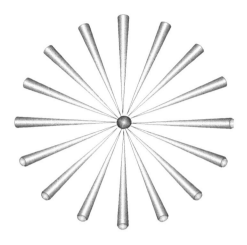

From each zero-point 16 cones
radiate outward in all directions.

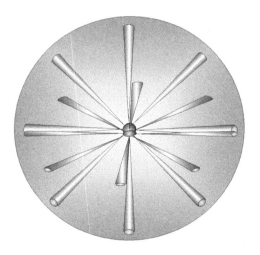

The zero-point as sphere gives rise to
16 cones in three dimensions.

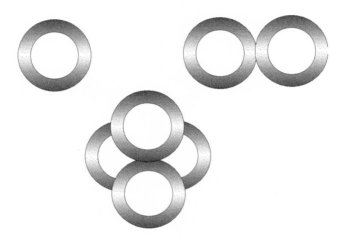

The zero can be twisted once to give two zeros (like a figure-eight) and each zero twisted again to give four.

If every zero is four zeros, each of the four can again produce four more, giving a set of 16 zeros.

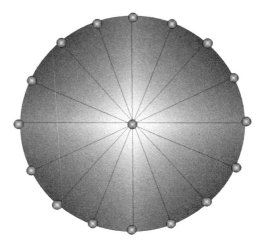

16 points surrounding a zero-point
define another zero.

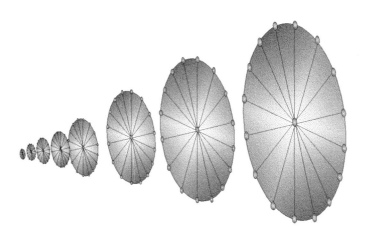

The zero-point expands into a cone shape
while remaining both zero and 16.

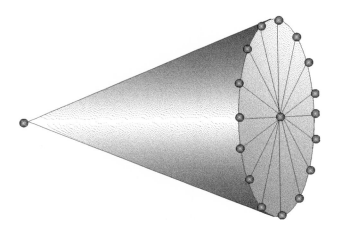

A cone forms as zero expands
along the baseline.

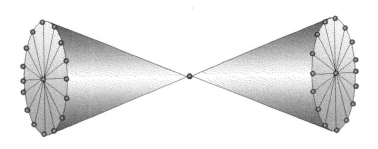

Cones may emerge not only from the front side of zero,
but also from the back side of zero.

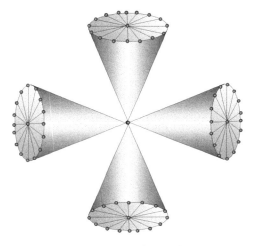

As cones emerge in four directions,
zero gives birth to 16 zero-points x 4 or 64 zeros.

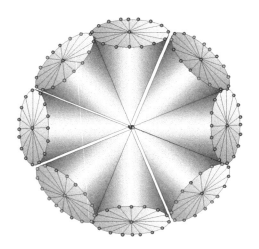

With the development of cones in eight directions,
zero gives birth to 16 zero-points x 8 or 128 zeros.

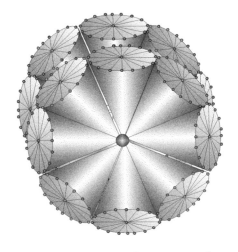

With the full development of 16 cones from one zero,
zero gives birth to 16 zero-points x 16 or 256 zeros.

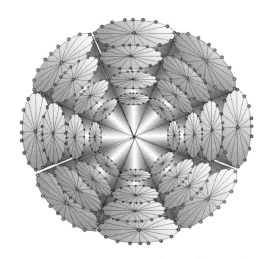

Two sets of 16 cones aligned together
create half of a large sphere.

Each cone is filled with smaller cones
branching in all directions from zero-points.

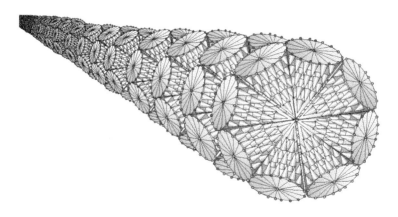

Long cones of cones filled with cones
extend from a single zero-point.

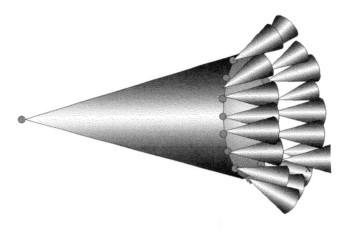

The 16 zero-points on the face of each cone
give rise to 16 cones.

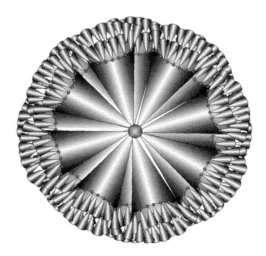

From a single zero-point 16 cones emerge in 16 directions, each in turn giving rise to 16 smaller cones.

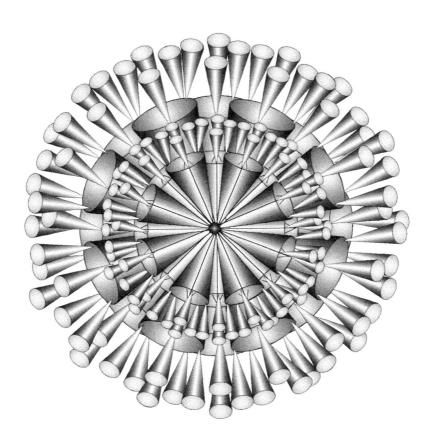

As zero gives 16 and 16 gives zeros that give 16,
forms fill all directions.

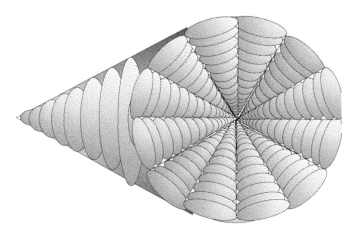

Each cone could develop in 16 ring-like stages,
each stage filled with smaller cones.

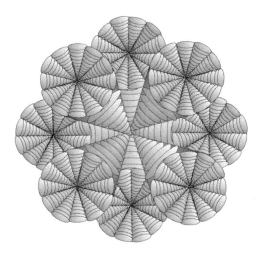

Eight cones with 16 rings emerge from one side of zero
while another eight cones might emerge from the back.

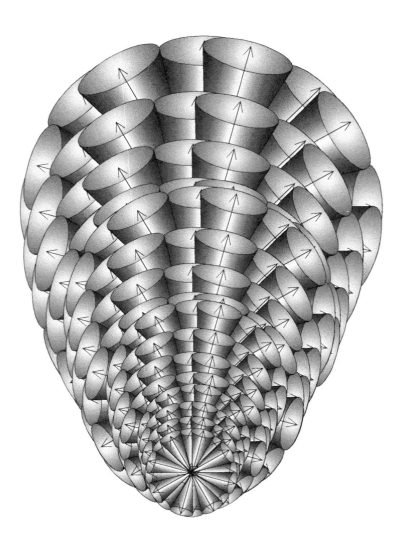

16 stages of development in a cone give 16 rings,
each made of layers of cones.

Oriented in four directions, cones arising
from zeros create endless patterns—cones of cones.

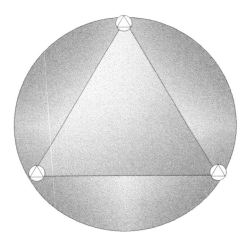

A moment of time: past, present, and future points all
have a past-present-future structure.

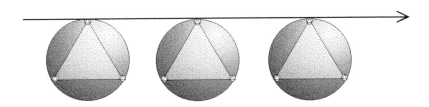

Each moment of time in a linear series might have
past-present-future structure and depth.

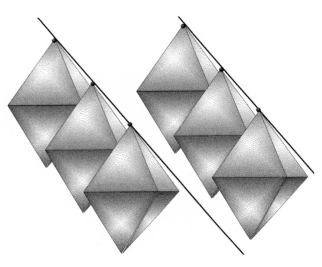

Taken to depth, triangles become faces of diamonds whose topmost points appear to flow in a linear series.

Deeper structure of diamonds might show four diamonds emerging from a single point.

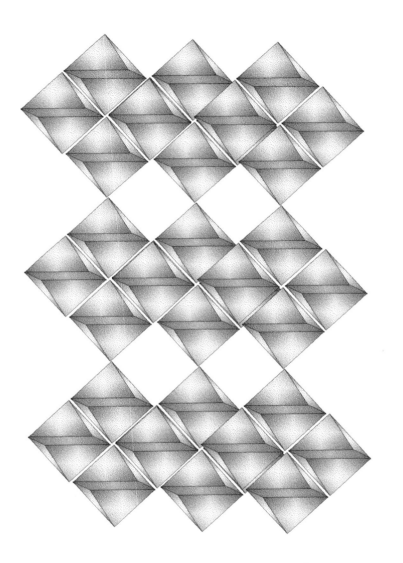

Linear series give way to a network
of diamonds in all directions.

Interchange of cones and diamonds.

Diamond structures appear within
the patterning of cones in all directions.

Resources

Time, Space, and Knowledge: A New Vision of Reality (1977) The root text of the TSK vision. Bold and visionary, it communicates the sense of discovery that marked the introduction of the vision. A series of thirty-five exercises are carefully structured to introduce the vision and allow readers to investigate it. This book has sold well for over forty years and has been widely adopted for classroom use in a variety of disciplines.

Knowledge of Freedom: Time to Change (1984) While not a part of the TSK vision, *Knowledge of Freedom* is a powerful guide to the structures of lower-level knowledge. Tracing the patterns of human existence, personal growth, and the operations of mind, it offer a 'universal autobiography', and introduces the power of knowledge to bring about transformation.

Love of Knowledge (1987)   A carefully reasoned exploration that has been of special interest for those with a strong academic background. In his introduction, Tarthang Tulku wrote: "Love of Knowledge proceeds by returning to a point 'before the beginning'—tracing out links between space, time, and knowledge and our ordinary understanding. The presentation inquires primarily into the structures of conventional, 'first-level' thought. Only when these structures have been identified and analyzed does the focus shift to a 'higher' level of knowledge." The reader is invited to explore fifty different exercises, crafting a personal path of inquiry.

Knowledge of Time and Space (1990)   In contrast to the more rigorous presentation of *Love of Knowledge* and the focused exposition found in *Time, Space, and Knowledge,* this work displays the flashing, penetrating presence of knowledge as it operates throughout time and space. Elegant and luminous, deeply artistic in the way it plays with knowledge, time, and space, this book provides an opportunity for active participation in creativity. Organized into more than a hundred short chapters that at times read almost like aphorisms, it offers countless starting points for inquiry.

Visions of Knowledge: Liberation of the Modern Mind (1993)   Speculations and essays relating to TSK, published as part of the Perspectives in Time, Space, Knowledge series. Sixty questions at the beginning of the book, each with commentary, help clarify the nature of TSK inquiry as a relaxed but always stimulating exploration. The book includes a detailed outline of *Knowledge of Time and Space,* keyed to related parts of other books, as well as short comments by students of the vision.

Dynamics of Time and Space: Transcending Limits on Knowledge (1994)   A fresh approach to the TSK vision that has drawn extensive praise from readers and reviewers. The discussion is deeply engaging and accessible, and the exercises open new dimensions of experience with surprising ease. A central focus in the exercises related to time is the nature of pain and how to work with it, which readers have found a remarkably fruitful approach.

More TSK- related books follow the index

Index

OTHER BOOKS

Dimensions of Thought I and II (1980)

A two volume set of thirteen essays by early readers of *Time, Space, and Knowledge*. Many of the essays explore connections with Western philosophy and psychology. A lengthy interview with Tarthang Tulku in Volume I provides one of the best short introductions to TSK. Volume II includes numerous short reports by readers.

Mastery of Mind (1993)

This volume of essays by long-term TSK students shows a decided shift away from theory and comparisons toward practical applications. Among the articles: A noted astronomer reflects on the challenge that TSK poses to science; a summary of a Ph.D. thesis on therapeutic applications of TSK, with thoughts from the thesis adviser on ways to improve such research in the future; a systems theorist suggests how TSK might revolutionize his field.

Light of Knowledge: Essays on the Interplay of Knowledge, Time, and Space (1997)

Philosophers, psychologists, meditators, and systems theorists explore the new paradigm for human experience made available in the TSK vision. The eleven articles, including an illuminating essay by Tarthang Tulku, show how the prevailing climate of skepticism and mistrust can be transformed into creative inquiry that has the power to break through limits.

A New Way of Being: Encounters, Engagements, Explorations, and Applications (2004).

Twenty-three practitioners introduce the TSK vision by showing its unfolding. Some have applied TSK to their professions or fields, and others have formed study groups to share their thoughts, experiences, and questions in dialogue.

A New Kind of Knowledge: Evocations, Exhibitions, Extensions, and Excavations (2004).

Seventeen students of the TSK Vision demonstrate forms of inquiry that can illuminate our lives. Penetrating reflections on knowledge, time, and experience, as well as practical applications in psychology, teaching, business, and time management.

When It Rains, Does Space Get Wet? Living the TSK Vision, by Jack Petranker (2006).

A systematic guide to the TSK Vision by one of its long-time practitioners. Innovative approaches, including a comprehensive 36-unit study program, a guide in 75 topics, notes on the TSK methodology, and over 100 pages summarizing the six books in the series.

Inside Knowledge: How to Activate the Radical New Vision of Reality Presented to the World by Tibetan Lama Tarthang Tulku: Edited essays, with an introduction and orientations by Jack Petranker (2015).

This book collects six essays by Tarthang Tulku and five contributions by serious students into an organic whole. Each essay is introduced by the editor, giving the volume a coherent approach. Many of the materials are difficult to find elsewhere. Twelve exercises drawn from the TSK books have been chosen to complement the readings. An accessible and engaging introduction to the TSK Vision.

ADDITIONAL RESOURCES

All books related to TSK can be found at www.dharma-publishing.com. Another website devoted to TSK and its applications can be found at www.creativeinquiry.org, which maintains an active forum. The Center for Creative Inquiry has also published several short works related to TSK: NowHere: an interactive workbook; Invisible Mind, and Full Presence Mindfulness: A Pocket Companion. Visit https://shop.creativeinquiry.org/

The Center for Creative Inquiry, founded in 2000, is inspired by and rooted in the TSK Vision. It presents retreats, workshops, and online programs in TSK and its off-shoot, Full Presence Mindfulness. Classes in TSK are also offered at Dharma College (www.dharma-college.com) and the Nyingma Institute, Berkeley (nyingmainstitute.com), and there are study groups in the US, the UK, Germany, and Israel. For more information contact cci@creativeinquiry.org.